Philippines 2025.

The sale of babies for adoption both here and abroad is now the country's biggest industry. It is not only legitimate but has the full backing of the government that sees it as an answer to the rapidly growing population. With business booming, not surprisingly, the number of illegal traders and baby thefts has also risen significantly.

The adoption angle may be true locally but globally, there's another story being told. Most are hawked as sources of food, medical parts and specimens for scientific research.

Beyond the moral bankruptcy of it, there's one issue about this system that has elicited a wave of public outcry. Though you may be the biological progeny of a baby, you are not recognized as its parent nee owner unless you and the child have the government-issued C.H.I.P. - Child's Home Identification Program - a microchip implant that verifies your claim. Without it, or with a bogus CHIP, you risk not only losing your baby but even face serious jail time.

Freddie and Freda - a childless couple - are thrust into this situation when a baby mysteriously lands at their doorstep one night. How the infant escaped the preying hands of thieves is beyond comprehension. This leads the cancer-stricken Freda to believe the baby is a gift from God with much opposition naturally from Freddie. But Freddie gives in to his wife's wishes after Freda bargains to keep the child for only thirty days - the maximum grace period allowed by law for anyone in possession of missing or stolen infants to return the "merchandise" to the authorities.

The child turns out to be a tremendous blessing. Now, they want to keep the baby for good; even if this means constantly dodging questions or suspicions from sneaky neighbors, eager to snitch on them for a government reward..

But their world of trouble takes on a more perilous spin when they are suddenly confronted by a checkered past that could put their whole future in jeopardy.

MIRACLE BABY

Screenplay by:

Natzee AB

Miracle Baby: A Screenplay by Natzee A B

Copyright © 2020. All rights reserved.

Published by Pen It! Publications, LLC in the U.S.A.
812-371-4128 www.penitpublications.com

ISBN: 978-1-952011-05-4
Edited by Rachel Hale
Cover Design by Donna Cook

FADE IN:

ARCHIVAL NEWS CLIP –

Protesters and activists, composed mostly of professionals, rant, chant and tersely wave their banner **A.N.A.K.*** outside the building headquarters of BABY CARE.

(*Note: Anak in Tagalog means "child". The acronym plays on that)

A Lexus roars out of the building's basement parking and grazes through a throng of news reporters peeling them away. Both activists and reporters give chase as it speeds off.

> FEMALE NEWSCASTER (VO)
> Members of the *Alyansa laban sa Nagbebentang Anak sa Kadupangan* (Alliance Against Infant Commerce) or A.N.A.K. held another protest rally outside the Baby Care Corporation headquarters. Baby Care is one of the biggest government-licensed companies engaged in infant adoption, an industry that has grown globally in recent years.

> SMASH CUT:

YOUTUBE VIDEO:

A stealth video showing the goings-on inside –

BABY CARE "Nurturing Facility"

A worker from inside the facility rolls out a wide wheelbarrow stacked with four non-transparent EZ boxes slapped with Baby Care's logo. More loaded wheelbarrows roll out in succession. The boxes are then loaded to a waiting delivery truck.

> MALE NEWSCASTER (VO)
> But reliable sources from ANAK say the company's operations allegedly extend beyond selling adoption rights.

EXT. SHANGHAI RESTAURANT/ALLEY - NIGHT

A huge wheelbarrow is rolled past the back-door kitchen of the
establishment, loaded with non-transparent EZ boxes similar to
Baby Care minus the logo that appears ostensibly scraped off.

Super: "Shanghai"

                    FEMALE NEWSCASTER (VO)
                It is widely believed that China is one of
                Baby Care's biggest markets. However, there are
                still no confirmed reports as to whether these
                Baby Care infants have found suitable homes
                here, considering China's ever-growing population
                problem.

KITCHEN - CONTINUOUS

Kitchen crew members yank off the lids from the boxes to reveal
lifeless, newly born infants bunched and stacked together in
each box. A crew member hauls out three of the merchandise,
lines them on a wide white-tiled island, and then hoses them to
sterilize. After the dead infants have been sufficiently doused,
he drops the hose then trades this for a huge cleaver like those
used in slasher films. Cam pans away as cleaver plunges on an
infant.

                    MALE NEWSCASTER (VO)
                Rumors abound on social media that due to
                the last major outbreak two years ago in
                the country – that saw its livestock and poultry
                significantly decimated, it is suspected
                that it has turned to these Philippine babies as
                sources for their survival.

DINING AREA - ANOTHER NIGHT

Two waiters emerge from the kitchen hoisting trays of sumptuous
meat dishes on each hand and deliver them to a big table
composed of American and Chinese businessmen. The ravenous
executives quickly dive into the plates as soon they land on the
table.

MALE NEWSCASTER (VO)
Online rumors abound that these imports have
become viable meat alternatives to pricey
delectable fare such as "Tender Beef Stew" and
"Fragile Soup 15". Baby Care was quick to deny
allegations that they were selling their
merchandise to the Chinese for purposes of
consumption.

ARCHIVAL CNN NEWS CLIP -

A.N.A.K., bunched with other human rights organizations, raises
their banners of dissent and vociferous voices outside the gates
of Malacañang Palace.

FEMALE NEWSCASTER (VO)
Members of A.N.A.K. together with other human
rights organizations staged another rally
outside Malacañang demanding the abolition
of Senate Bill code-named Baby Boom…

CUT TO:

INT. PHILIPPINE SENATE - ARCHIVAL FOOTAGE

Camera pans to the faces of Senators, both corpulent and aging.
Most of them were former showbiz personalities - starlets and
comedians hosting noontime shows and action stars.

FEMALE NEWSCASTER (VO)
…that legalizes the purchase and sale of
abandoned or relinquished infants by authorized
corporations. The bill seeks to address the ever-
pressing problem of so-called "Garbage Infants"
among the country's marginalized that had grown
in alarming numbers over the last decade or so.
In an effort to ease their burdens, the bill
allows them to sell their new-born to authorized
corporations rather than discard them. Before the
bill was passed, it was reported that hundreds
upon hundreds of these abandoned infants were
uncovered in various dumping grounds all over the
country.

CUT TO:

ARCHIVAL CNN NEWS CLIP -

There is a long queue of these marginalized - solo parents or couples clutching their new-born - outside the Baby Boom headquarters, waiting to sell their infants.

                         MALE NEWSCASTER (VO)
                 Since its implementation, the bill has
                 likewise alleviated the burdens on social
                 welfare agencies forced to turn away a great
                 number of these infants due to budgetary
                 concerns. Over the last decade Baby Boom has
                 escalated into the fastest-growing industry in
                 the country. However, with overseas demand
                 growing rapidly in numbers, a number of
                 unlicensed traders willing to drop prices have
                 joined the fray, giving the legitimate outlets
                 stiff competition.

                                      CUT TO:

EXT. BINONDO COMMERCIAL BUILDING - LATE NIGHT

A reed-thin and slovenly woman, clutching a heavy athletic bag against her chest, stops by the shut accordion-style metal gate of one commercial unit that had closed for the day. She punches the doorbell while swivelling both ways to check if anyone had followed or was watching her. When the doorbell fails to summon someone from inside, she rattles the accordion gate.

                        WOMAN
                 (Whispered screams)
            Singian… Singian!

Soon we hear footsteps pounding down a staircase. The gates slide brusquely to one side. A corpulent Chinese man, in his early forties and slightly balding, is revealed standing behind it. He juts out of the doorway and swivels both ways to check if anyone was watching them before hurriedly ushering the woman inside. He shuts the gates and gesticulates that she follows him upstairs that leads to -

A SHABBY AND STUFFY ROOM -

Chinese fat guy tells the woman to unload the "merchandise" from her bag.

> FEMALE NEWSCASTER (VO)
> As the baby industry continues to boom, the number of cases of "Baby Piracy" has also risen to alarming proportions.

The woman unzips the bag and hauls out a new-born that's fast asleep, quite possibly drugged, similar to what syndicates would do with infant props for panhandlers. The woman hoists the child for the Chinese to examine. Satisfied, he tells her to lay the infant inside an EZ box with a fabricated Baby Care logo. He whips out his wallet and forks over a few lousy hundreds to her. She glumly looks at the money and pleads for more. He gives her a stern "take it or leave it" look. She reluctantly takes the cash.

> FEMALE NEWSCASTER (VO)
> This is so because according to the law, any baby vendor, regardless of whether single or married, is allowed to sell a maximum of only two babies to any licensed trader. It is widely believed that those with more to offer have resorted to selling their babies to unauthorized operators.

ARCHIVAL BBC NEWS CLIP –

Three members of Special Law Enforcement Unit on Trade Hazards or SLEUTH – Infant Crime Division, better known as **"Baby Police,"** on social media flank a man with a suspicious duffel bag. They sport uniforms similar to the Nazis but in baby blue colors. The man with the bag tries to flee but the three are quick to fence him in.

> MALE NEWSCASTER (VO)
> Along with baby piracy, incidence of baby theft has also risen significantly in such a short period…

ARCHIVAL BBC NEWS CLIP –

Pan to new-borns in a hospital nursery. Two-armed SECURITY GUARDS man the entrance.

                    MALE NEWSCASTER (VO)
          Some of these babies have been allegedly
          snatched from nurseries of both government and
          private hospitals. The government has ordered
          all hospitals to enforce more stringent measures
          to ensure the safety of these infants.

ARCHIVAL LOCAL NEWS CLIP -

Interview with a Baby Police identified as the Chief of SLEUTH -
Infant Crime Division

                    BABY POLICE CHIEF
          We encourage the public in cooperating with us.
          Should they have information regarding stolen
          infants please notify us immediately. There is a
          reward for any information leading to the
          recovery of these missing infants. For those that
          have bought stolen babies from unauthorized
          dealers or obtained them by some other means,
          please be warned that you have until thirty days
          to surrender the baby or babies. Those caught
          will be subject to the full extent of the law.

TV NEWS -

A banner appears at the bottom of the screen: *Today's News -
April 29, 2025*

A thirty-ish, sophisticated and good-looking however distraught
mother weeps before the cameras while hoisting the picture of a
new-born baby.

                    MOTHER
          I am appealing to the public to help us find our
          adopted son. We lost him last night at the
          hospital where he was confined. I am offering a
          reward in addition to what the government is
          offering to anyone who can return him to us soon.
          He is wearing a tag with the initials AM.
          His name is Anthony Mendez…

SCREEN GOES BLACK AS SOMEONE SHUTS THE TV OFF.

                        WOMAN'S VOICE (VO)
                   So, what's your blessing this week? Any
                   good news? Anyone?

INT. PASTOR'S HOUSE - NIGHT

A group of women, categorized in their Born-Again circles as
Discipleship Group or D-Group Ladies, are gathered around a
large dining table. The one whose voice we just heard is leading
the group discussion. She's the PASTOR'S WIFE, mid-fifties,
voluptuous but smartly garbed.

One of the ladies, mid-thirties, raises her hand, grinning from
ear-to-ear.

                        PASTOR'S WIFE
                   Yes Bing. What's your story?

                        LADY 1
                   Yes. Praise God. And thank you all for
                   your prayers. We came from the doctor
                   this afternoon.

Everybody's excited faces hang on what she will say next.

                        PASTOR'S WIFE
              And?

                        LADY 1
                   God is truly amazing. I'm having a baby!

Applause and "Praise God" erupt. Everyone around the table seems
genuinely happy for her save for one by the corner leaning
against the cupboard - FREDA, who is only a couple of years shy
of 40 yet looks much older due to the weight of the world on her
shoulders. Still, she manages to offer an obligatory smile when
the expectant mother turns her way.

                        SMASH CUT:

DOCTOR'S CLINIC - FLASHBACK

FREDA and husband FREDDIE, about her age or younger, listen
glumly to their GYNECOLOGIST.

                    GYNECOLOGIST
          I'm sorry Mrs. Mangahis. But what you
          have is pseudocyesis or what is commonly
          known as hysterical pregnancy.

She refuses to look up from the floor. Tears stream down her
cheeks. Freddie takes her hand and squeezes it reassuringly.

                    GYNECOLOGIST
          I know how hard this must be for you.
          You've been trying for so long.

                    FREDA
          I know. It's hysterical, right?

                    GYNECOLOGIST
          Have you considered fertility treatment?
          I can recommend a specialist. She's a friend
          of mine. She's very good. She has a very high
          success rate.

                    FREDA
          And she must be very expensive.

                    GYNECOLOGIST
          Well…I'm sure something can be arranged.

                    FREDA
                    (to Freddie)
          What do you think, hon? You think something
          can be arranged?

Freddie breathes hard and smiles. Cam stays on him highlighting
the huge SCAR on his forehead.

PASTOR'S HOUSE - END OF FLASHBACK

The D-Group ladies nosh on junk food while exchanging plenty of
laughs. All are in on the revelry except FREDA.

                    LADY 2
          I'd be careful if I were you. You can't be
          too sure about hospitals these days. Have

you seen the news? About baby robberies
going on there?

                    LADY 1
I think that's only in government hospitals.

                    LADY 3
Ha! Have you been to one? I don't think
nurseries even exist there. We're talking all
hospitals now. Even the big ones where you
thought you're safe.

                    LADY 1
That's awful.

                    LADY 3
There are rumors that some nurses and orderlies
are in cahoots with these thieves. You can't
blame them. Their pay is pathetic.

                    LADY 4
Well…had I known ten years ago that you could
sell your babies like hotcakes, I would have put
off that ligation.

                    LADY 5
In Europe, there are rumors that these
babies are treated like lab monkeys.
They cut them up and take out the organs for
various experiments.

                    LADY 1
What? How can our government agree to that?

                    LADY 5
Well, they don't. Supposedly. They blame the
Baby Pirates from Binondo for all this.

                    LADY 1
You think they really do that in Europe?

                         SMASH CUT:

EXT. BACK ALLEY - NIGHT

SUPER: *"ROMANIA"* – Dumpsters are teeming with eviscerated bodies of babies.

>   LADY 5 (VO)
>   You know what else I hear? After they're
>   done with these babies, they dump them like
>   sanitary napkins in dumpsters. No arrests made.
>   No cease and deceased orders from their
>   government.

>   LADY 1(VO)
>   What's happening with our world?

>   LADY 4 (VO)
>   So Katz, (Lady 1)…You still wanna have
>   that baby?

                                        CUT BACK TO:

FREDA AND THE LADIES -

Protests, banter, chuckles erupt. FREDA remains silent and stoic.

>   PASTOR'S WIFE
>   Alright. Enough with the baby horror
>   stories. Is there anybody else who would
>   like to share?

Freda limply raises her hand.

>   PASTOR'S WIFE
>   Yes, Freda?

>   FREDA
>   Me, I'm also positive.

The ladies erupt with taunts i.e. "Positive? As in positively insane?" Chuckles erupt. Pastor's Wife shushes them.

>   PASTOR'S WIFE
>   Wow! Positive as in you're also preggy?

>   FREDA
>   Nope. Positive for Stage 2 breast cancer.

Sympathetic "Awwww", both genuine and hokey, spills out from everyone.

That draws the attention of the husbands, or the D-Group men, holding their own Bible discussion, from the adjacent dining area, particularly FREDDIE. Judging from his reactions, it's obvious Freda's revelation is news to him as well.

EXT. WET MARKET IN MANDALUYONG - SAME NIGHT

An AETA (indigenous person from Zambales) wanders about, perhaps looking from some reprieve from the huge and tattered eco bag slung on her shoulder, which she protects with both hands.

She rushes to a shadowy corner as a Baby Police squad van rolls past her.

VAN'S REARVIEW MIRROR -

The Aeta emerges from the shadows and shuffles off to the opposite direction from whence she came. As she hurries off, her bag WIGGLES as if what's inside it wants to pop out.

The VAN screeches to a halt and drives backward.

VAN PULLS OVER -

A BABY POLICE hops out with a black gadget that looks like a credit card terminal. The woman shuffles off even as her bag wiggles.

                    BABY POLICE 1
              Hey lady, stop. I said stop!

The woman refuses to heed and scurries off.

Baby's cry explodes from inside her bag.

EXT. RESIDENTIAL COMPOUND/PASTOR'S HOUSE - SAME NIGHT

The D-Group ladies hug each other good night. The D-Group men shake hands, pat each other on the back as they bid farewell. Then they peel off -

The other couples head to their cars while FREDA and FREDDIE walk their way to the community gate. They're the only couple in the group that's not only childless but car-less as well.

EXT. BONI AVENUE - LATER

Their group mates 'cars wheeze by them, one after another. They put on fake smiles and wave at them. Not a single car stops to offer them a ride. Jeepneys fly by but far in between. FREDDIE flags each one but they don't stop for them.

He flags down another one coming their way. Through the windshield, he sees the driver waving no more room.

An empty cab follows that and slows down as if telling the couple that he's taking passengers. FREDA shakes her head thanks but no. Cab rolls away.

                    FREDDIE
              (Eye on the road)
          When were you planning on telling me?

She shrugs indifferently.

                    FREDA
          Waiting for the right time.

                    FREDDIE
          When? After telling everyone else first?

                    FREDA
          When you're not tired and grumpy like
          you are now.

She could tell by his silence what's really going on in his mind.

                    FREDA
          Go ahead. I know what you want to ask me.

                    FREDDIE
          How…?

                        FREDA
          How are we going to pay for this...sssh…?
          Oh yeah. God. Who else, right? Remember what
          He said?
                    (chuckles mockingly)
          "Be still and know that I am God." He knows
          our every need. So, all we have to do is pray
          and he'll take care of everything, right?

                        FREDDIE
          Hmmm. You don't believe prayer works?

                        FREDA
          Oh, I'll believe it. If he starts answering mine.
                    (Rocks head to the heavens)
          God, you know what's the problem? You're
          all talk, talk, pray, pray, trust,
          trust, trust. Well, here's the thing. Trust is
          good but cash is better. Especially now that
          we're going to need plenty of it.

Another jeepney wheezes by. This time it's her turn to flag it
down. The jeepney slows down but the driver signals there's only
room for one more.

                        FREDDIE
          That's okay. Get in.

She squeezes inside while he hangs by the jeepney's rear or
stirrup. In Pinoy commuting culture, this is known as *"sabit"*
(hang).

EXT. SHAW BOULEVARD - SAME NIGHT

They alight from the jeepney and witness a commotion going on at
the entrance to the street where they live.

The same Squad Van we saw earlier, WANG-WANGs (their siren is
that of a baby wailing in tears) and then pulls over where the
commotion is happening.

The FEMALE AETA is clutching a wailing baby in her arms that
came from her bag. The baby has her complexion and fizzy hair.
She has a knife against baby's neck.

Two unarmed BABY POLICE, who have caught up with her, accost her
with caution with their hands raised, gesturing to put the knife
down. Another member of their team leaps out of the van with a
SHOTGUN ready to blow her to flesh chunks.

The one with the black gadget signals to Shotgun Man to get back
in the van and stay put. He slowly accosts the Aeta, hand raised
as if assuring her he is no threat. She is not buying his puppy-
dog appeal and backs off with every step he takes.

                    BABY POLICE 1
          Please. Don't make this any worse for you.
          Keep that knife away from the baby.

                    AETA WOMAN
          Why? So you can steal him from me?
          He's my son! Look. Does he look like he
          came from somebody else's *puday? (*Note: Tagalog
          slang for vagina)

                    BABY POLICE 1
          We're just following the law here, lady.
          If that kid's really yours, bring him to
          us so we can check.

                    BABY POLICE 2
          If that kid has a C.H.I.P. we all go home
          happy. I swear.

                    AETA WOMAN
          CHIP? What CHIP? We have nothing to eat and you
          want us buy CHIP? What shit is that? This is my
          son, my flesh and blood, and you're taking him
          because he has no CHIP?

She spots Shotgun Man taking careful aim at her now. She buries
the blade deeper into her baby's neck. The child screams in
pain.

BABY POLICE 2 yells at his companion to put down the gun. BABY
POLICE 1 marches slowly while she continues to back off, blade
still on the child, her eyes seething with rage.

                    BABY POLICE 1
          Please, I'm not going to hurt you. Just
          keep the knife away from that baby.

Seemingly, the woman relents as she pulls the knife away from the child and lowers her hand. She kisses him on the forehead. Just when the Baby Police are lowering their guard as well…

She rocks her head up to the skies, as if apologizing for what she's about to do before swinging the knife back on the baby's neck. Baby Police 1 launches forward in sheer panic.

                    AETA WOMAN
          You want my son?
                    (pause)
          Here, take him.

She SLASHES the baby's neck then tosses him over to Baby Police 1. He drops his black gadget as he tries to catch the baby. Blood smears on his uniform.

The woman flees, now much swifter on her feet and makes a turn to the perpendicular street. Baby Police 2 promptly gives chase.

Baby Police 1 bends to pick up his gadget and rushes the bleeding-to-death infant to the van. He barks at Shotgun Man to move aside as he hops on. Door slides and shuts close.

FREDDIE yanks FREDA'S arm.

                    FREDDIE
          Let's go.

She relents but unable to resist glancing back at the tattered bag where the bleeding baby was kept.

INT. SQUAD VAN -

SHOTGUN MAN looks on as BABY POLICE 1 lowers the convulsing-for-life baby inside ice box. Not long after, the baby stops convulsing, losing its battle to survive.

                    SHOTGUN MAN
          Sonamagun! Is that still usable?

                    BABY POLICE 1
          Yes. But we only have one hour before it spoils.
          Call Richard. Tell him to give up the *baluga**
          and haul his ass back here.

(*pejorative term for Aeta)

EXT. APARTMENT COMMON AREA - SAME NIGHT

We pass a row of roach-and-rodent ramshackle apartments built in
the 60s - a common sight in lower middle-class neighborhoods.

FREDDIE and FREDA mosey past the units as they head for theirs
at the cul de sac.

THEIR POV -

All their neighbors, however exhausted, are still up, caring for
their infants or toddlers still awake.

INT. FREDDIE & FREDDA'S UNIT - SAME NIGHT

ON TV: NATIONAL STATISTICS OFFICE INFOMERCIAL (NSO)

NSO Chairman *WILLIE REVILLAME is on cam.

(*Note: Revillame is a popular TV personality in the
Philippines)

                         WILLIE
                Since the Child's Home Identification
                Program or…

C.H.I.P. logo flashes

                         WILLIE (VO)
                C.H.I.P. was launched, there has been a
                remarkable improvement…

We finally see what C.H.I.P is all about - a microchip injected
into the arm of a newly born infant.

                         WILLIE (VO)
                In providing the public maximum protection…

C.H.I.P is also administered to the biological (or adoptive)
parents of a child.
                         WILLIE (VO)
                …from massive child piracy and theft…

MONTAGE: NEWS CLIPS - Arrested "Baby Pirates" by the Infant Crime Unit.

                    WILLIE (VO)
               ...thanks also, in no small measure, to
               the efforts of the SLEUTH - Infant Crime
               division.

A couple hoists their baby to a Baby Police clutching the same black gadget we saw with Baby Police 1 earlier, except this one comes with a laser gun extension similar to checking bar codes. This is called a BIOSCANNER. The couple looks approvingly as the Baby Police aims and guns the Bio-Scanner in the infant's eyes. After he's done with the child, he points gun at parents (categorically called - "Child Proprietors")

                    WILLIE (VO)
               The C.H.I.P ensures that the child you claim
               is yours is registered under your names. This
               eliminates potential disputes regarding
               ownership of the child.

ON THE BIOSCANNER LCD -

 "REGISTERED TO MR & MRS. OCAMPO" lights up.

Baby Police smiles with confirmation. The relieved couple smiles back.

                    WILLIE (VO)
               So, if you or your child doesn't have a C.H.I.P.
               yet, make sure to drop by an NSO Center
               nearest to you.

ON WILLIE:

                    WILLIE
               Remember…with C.H.I.P., your baby's yours
               to keep.

ON FREDDIE - wincing in disgust at the infomercial

                    FREDDIE
               Revillame is such a blowhard. I'm sure he'd
               have no qualms selling your soul wholesale to

                    the Chinese if he could...

FREDA, by the dining table, is barely tuned in to him as she
lazily sips her coffee and nearly dissolving her furtive tears
with it.

FREDDIE soon takes notice of her waterworks. He gently caresses
her back to mollify her.

                    FREDDIE
          I don't know why you do this. You cry as if I
          don't care. Even Pastor Roger was surprised why
          I didn't know about it. The group could have
          prayed about it sooner.

                    FREDA
          It's not this stupid cancer I'm crying about.

                    FREDDIE
          No? What then?

                    FREDA
          Bing. Do you know that she's pregnant?

                    FREDDIE
          I heard. That's what's killing you?

                    FREDA
          Bing and I are the only childless ladies
          in the group. Dya know that?
                    (parodying a sports anchor's voice)
          And then there was one, folks.
                    (pause)
          One freakin' baby. Just one to make
          my life complete.
                         (tears streaming
                         down again)
          That's all I ever asked from God.
                    (pause)
          Now that prayer's going to die with me.

ON TV:

BABY SHAMPOO COMMERCIAL PLAYS

Baby giggles that drive you mad while shampoo suds bubble on his cheeks.

                    FREDA (VO)
          I can't have riches. I can't have my
          own house. And I can't have a baby.

ON FREDA -

                    FREDA
          My God! Why is my life such a big joke?

ON TV:

A PINOY TELESERYE RESUMES -

A teen couple lugubriously face each other under a tree. The girl is inconsolable. The boy's heart is throbbing with fear.

                    TEEN GUY
          What is it? Tell me?

                    TEEN GIRL
          Emeric, I'm pregnant.

                    TEEN BOY
          What? How?

TEEN GIRL is livid, triggering a heated exchange of words.

                    FREDA (VO)
          Oh, screw those teleseryes already. Why is it
          when some teen gets knocked up, it's like
          the end of the world?

BEDROOM - LATER

They lie in bed distant from each other, their backs facing each other. FREDDIE is curved in a fetal position, snoring off his daily troubles. FREDA turns to him. She's having difficulty nodding off. She reaches for her breast under her shirt where the malignant nodule is supposedly located. She grimaces in pain after pressing it.

IN FRONT OF THE MIRROR - LATER

She raises her shirt. The tumor on her breast is BIG. She holds
a shaving blade against it. She gulps air, perhaps mustering
strength to surgically extricate it when -

NGYAAAAW!!!

Cats, playing and rumbling on their precarious roof startle her.

                    FREDA
          Ssshhh…t!

The pesky strays hiss, screech and meow as they scamper off.

A baby's whimpering from the unit next to them wafts into the
room and mollifies her. Something about the baby's entreaty jogs
her memory. The baby hushes as his mother sings to him. Freda
lowers the blade and lowers her shirt.

                    FREDA (VO)
          God, you know it's not my fault. Why can't
          you forgive me?

The baby erupts in tearful cries, perhaps after the mother had
replaced him in his crib. Freda presses a finger against her lip
and shushes the infant.

                    FREDA (VO)
          Hush, baby. It's too early to cry in life.
          Cry later when someone stabs your back. Or
          someone breaks your heart. Or…
                    (pause)
          When God screws up your life for good.

DINING - NEXT MORNING

FREDA comes down and finds FREDDIE at the table, rifling through
credit card transaction receipts and punching up the total on
the calculator while listening to the radio. He sips coffee from
a mug with his name on it. There is a plate of pan de sal and
fried egg already set. Freddie looks up to acknowledge her.

ON RADIO:

                    ANNCR (VO)

In the headlines – NSO plans to release a more
affordable C.H.I.P. Is this C.H.I.P going to be
really cheap? Number of Baby Pirates continues to
rise. Are the Baby Police involved? An Aeta
bleeds dry an unregistered infant with a knife.
The Baby Police's response? No C.H.I.P., no
problemo.

She plants a morning kiss before taking her seat from across
him. He pushes the plate of food to her. She looks inquiringly
at him.

                    FREDDIE
          I've eaten. That's all yours.

He pulls Freda's mug with her name on it (yes, they have a pair
his and hers mugs)

                    FREDDIE
          Coffee?

She declines but instead pulls Freddie's mug to her then lazily
sips from it while assessing the pile of payables. She puts
down his cup and picks up one billing statement while forking a
slice of egg into her mouth.

ON RADIO – MORE HEADLINES

                    ANNCR (VO)
          A.N.A.K. and other human rights organizations
          will march again to Malacañang to demand the
          abolition of the Baby Trade Bill. The Senate's
          response? Hush now, A.N.A.K.

She replaces the billing statement on the pile.

                    FREDA
          Are we gonna be homeless soon?

He sips sullenly from his mug.

                    RADIO ANNCR (VO)
          And hold on to your seats for this
          one, people…Tonight's Super Lotto jackpot
          is now one hundred eighty million!

This announcement finally grabs their attention. Freddie's cell phone rings. He answers it.

                    FREDDIE
          Hello?…
                    (listens)
          Yes, speaking.
                    (listens)
          Uh-huh. What time tomorrow?
                    (listens)
          Uh-huh. Okay. See you. Bye.

Call ends. He's speechless. Freda stares, eager to yank out from him why.

                    FREDDIE
          It's that company I'm applying with.
          They want me to come tomorrow.

EXT. CENTRAL BUSINESS DISTRICT —THE NEXT DAY

Lunch break. People stream out of a huge building.

FREDDIE goes with the flow. His face is crumpled. Something tells you that interview didn't go too well.

EXT. EDSA CROSSING/FOOD KIOSK – LATER

FREDDIE, standing next to a donut stall, devours a donut in few quick bites. It doesn't fill him but he can't afford another.

He walks to a jeepney central where scores of passengers are already queuing up.

He passes by a Lotto outlet. The radio announcer got his numbers wrong. The pot is now a whopping TWO HUNDRED MILLION.

He draws one card but checks his cash situation in his pocket. He barely has enough for a ride home.

He flings the card to a nearby trash can.

INT. THEIR APARTMENT - LATER

FREDDIE arrives in time to catch FREDA about to have lunch. "How did it go" her eyes inquire. He flashes the thumb down sign.

BEDROOM - THAT NIGHT

Thunder peals. Rainfall pounds their fragile roof. Water seeping through their ceiling drips into a waiting pail by the foot of their bed.

FREDA lies awake on her back. FREDDIE is in his comfortable fetal position snoring today's blues away.

Above, she could again hear cats hissing, scampering on their roof and meowing cantankerously.

In the apartment unit bedroom adjacent to theirs, she could also hear a baby whining and screaming in concert with the cats. After a while their persistent noise establishes a certain dynamic. When the baby's voice recedes, the cats meowing cranks up and then vice versa.

This goes on for a while making it more difficult for Freda to catch Zzzs. As the cats volume recedes again, something breaks out from the cacophony.

It's the sound of ANOTHER BABY crying - not from next door or even from several doors away.

Freda lurches towards the window to check where it's coming from. Lightning cracks; thunder booms. She recoils.

LIVING ROOM - CONTINUOUS

The baby's whimpering and snivelling crescendos. Her heart thuds as she draws closer to the door.

The door creaks open. She gasps at the sight of -

OUTSIDE THEIR UNIT- CONTINUOUS

- A BABY wrapped in dirty blanket right outside their door. Raindrops skip and dance to keep the child from getting wet.

She looks sideways several times before picking up the child. He is barely drenched despite the splashing downpour.

As if sensing he's in safe hands now, child stops whimpering. His face gradually illumines like a newly lit lamp. Then he CACKLES, drowning the sound of the slashing, pounding rain.

Certain that no one is spying on her, FREDA hauls him inside.

MONTAGE -

1) She rifles through her closet and yanks out a set of baby clothes still sealed with the manufacturer's tag. A hanky, tucked to it drops to the floor. The hanky draws up some ambivalent reaction from her. She wipes the baby's forehead with it.
2) FREDA strips the baby of its soiled clothes.
3) She dusts off the thin film of dust on plastic pack before unwrapping the clothes.
4) She notices the baby still has a hospital tag strapped to his wrist. After reading it, she cuts the tag and tosses it into the laundry basket along with the soiled clothes and her unearthed hanky.

FREDA - LATER

She rocks the baby in her arms and tickles his nose with hers.

                    FREDA (VO)
          Oh Lord…
                    (pause)
          Thank you.

The baby cracks up. His creepy laughter sounds like that of an old man's. Freda is hardly perturbed.

BEDROOM - THE FOLLOWING DAY

FREDDIE wakes up without FREDA by her side.

He is alerted to a baby cackling below. He nervously hauls himself out of bed, races and stops midway down the stairs.

LIVING ROOM DOWNSTAIRS - CONTINUOUS

He leans by the banister, eyes popping out as he finds -

FREDA, rocking a baby in her arms. The baby chuckles as if
laughing at him.

                    FREDDIE
          Where'd you get that?

She approaches to show him her new bundle of loud joy.

                    FREDA
          Isn't he the cutest thing on earth?

                    FREDDIE
          Is that the pesky kid from next door?

She smiles, turns his back on him, as if ignoring his question.

                    FREDDIE
          Hon?

Baby whines, clamoring to be lulled to sleep. Freda sings as she
sways him.

                    FREDDIE
          Whose child is that?

She whips around, hushes him to keep his voice down.

                    FREDDIE
          Whose....?

                    FREDA
          Heaven's. This is God finally answering
          my prayers.

                    FREDDIE
          What?

                    FREDA
          I found him outside our door last night.
          An angel must have left him for us.

His blood pressure cranks up. He races to the window to check if anyone had been eavesdropping on them. Coast is clear. His paranoia ruffles her somewhat.

                    FREDA
          What's your problem?

He swivels from one section of the house to the next, desperately searching for something. A dirty blanket jutting out of their teeming laundry basket disrupts his flow. When he picks it up, he finds a cut-out hospital tag beneath it. He glares inquiringly at Freda after reading the tag while hoisting the soiled blanket at her.

                    FREDDIE
          Was he in this?

                    FREDA
          Yes.
                    FREDDIE
               (horrified)
          You better wrap him back in it.

                    FREDA
          And do what?

                    FREDDIE
          What?! We go to the Baby Poos and surrender that.

She snatches the blanket from him, causing him to drop the tag. She picks it up and deposits both articles in the trash bin.

                    FREDA
          No. We won't. Finders keepers.

                    FREDDIE
          Are you nuts! You want to go to prison?

The baby bawls. She races upstairs, cupping her hand on his mouth to muffle him. Freddie quickly follows suit.

THEIR ROOM - CONTINUOUS

She lays down the child in their bed and plays the boom box, cranking up the volume enough to drown the wailing infant. Then she joins him in bed and rocks his thighs to lull him to sleep.

                         FREDA
              Sssshhh. Daddy was just kidding.
                    (whispers to his ear)
              We're not giving you away. I swear.

The child is mollifie. Sobbing dials down to sniveling. She
hurls a dagger look at FREDDIE, shifting restlessly by the
doorway.

                         FREDDIE
              You're being stupid. Anyone who
              hears that kid…sssshh…t
                    (pause)
              We're screwed.

                         FREDA
                    (finger pressed against her lips)
              Sssshhh. The baby…

She hums a tune, "Wonderful Baby" by Don Mclean then lulls him
to sleep. The kid whimpers and then is off to dreamland. Freddie
is about to say something else, but she hoists her hand at him
to hold that thought. Sensing the baby's fast asleep now, she
gesticulates to keep their voices down.

                         FREDA
              If we get caught, I'll take full responsibility.
              You can just visit me in jail.

                         FREDDIE
              Ha-ha. Good you find this funny.

                         FREDA
              Think about it. Jail's not the worst that
              could happen. I could be dead next year for all
              you freakin' care.

He joins her in bed.

                         FREDDIE
              Can we have a sane discussion about this?
                    (pause)
              I know how badly you want this.
              But this is crazy.

The child's eyes pop open. He snivels as if responding to their conversation. Freda rocks his thighs then lulls him to sleep. The child yawns as his eyes drop.

They resume their conversation, their backs on the child. Something happens that eludes them both.

The child's face **LIGHTS UP** like a bulb.

>   FREDA
> You think I'm crazy? I'll tell you what's
> crazy. Here's me caring for this life, and I'm
> the criminal. What about those mothers
> selling theirbabies to those greedy Chekwas?*
> Now that's legal? God thinks it's okay too
> and does nothing? He is so unfair. He is so…
>   (tears crack up her voice)

>   FREDDIE
> You know that's not true. He said…

>   FREDA
> Yeah, yeah. He said this and he said that.
> That's all he does. All big talk.
>   (pause)
> Here we are…hoping, wishing, praying all these
> years even for just one and He doesn't care.

(* Note: Pinoy slur for Chinese)

He caresses her back and wipes her tears.

>   FREDA
> Dad, if I'm dying, I just want to enjoy whatever
> little time I have. I want to feel my life was at
> least worth something.
>   (pause)
> This baby…This baby makes it worth
> everything.

>   FREDDIE
> Supposed that were true, would you really
> like to spend your last days being some prison
> dike's bitch?

>   FREDA
> Hon, you know I've never asked for anything

much, right? But just this once,
I'm begging you, pleading you, please let me be
mother to this child. Even for a brief moment.
          (pause)
Forget about my treatment. Forget those medical
bills. This baby is worth more than all the
chemotherapy in the world.

                    FREDDIE
                    (sighs)
You know that's too much to ask…

                    FREDA
Please, dad. For me. Please.
                    (squeezes his hand as his head
                    drops in resigned silence)

                    FREDDIE
                    (Something hits him)
Wait…Wait. I just remembered something.
                    (pause)
Yes. That's it. Thirty days. They say if you
find a stray baby and surrender him within that
period, you're clear. No jail time. We might even
get a reward for it.

                    FREDA
Really? So, you're saying…?

                    FREDDIE
Thirty days. But that's it. Non-negotiable.
No extensions.

She joyfully wraps her hands around his face. In so doing, she
strokes the big scar on his forehead. He recoils. She ignores
this and kisses the scar anyway.

                    FREDA
Thank you.

He turns to the child who is smiling in his sleep as if pleased
with his decision.

                    FREDA
Look at our baby. I think he's saying
thank you too.

He rises and begins to make his way downstairs. He hasn't had breakfast yet.

                         FREDA
              Hon...

He pauses by the door and turns.

                         FREDA
              You know I'd breastfeed him if I could, right?

INT. GROCERY - ANOTHER DAY

FREDDIE picks up a big can of powdered baby's milk. He checks the shelf for the price and winces at how expensive it is.

A woman walks past him, pushing a baby carriage. She smiles at him as he examines the can. He reciprocates gesture then peeked in her carriage. There's a chubby and cute baby girl in it.

The woman tiptoes to reach for a big can of milk from the top shelf. Freddie assists her and even lands the can in her cart. She signals if he could fetch him another.

After the woman thanks him and strolls away, he proceeds to pick up the smaller can of the same brand she got.

EXT. GROCERY - LATER

FREDDIE waits for a jeepney ride. The woman he helped stands a few paces away from him. The grocery bags of milk are saddled up behind the carriage that's before her. She tries to flag down a cab, but it is occupied.

A tinted FX vehicle* emerges from a perpendicular street and turns to the main thoroughfare. It slows down and pulls over right where the woman with her baby carriage is standing. A brawny man in tank tops and tattoos on his shoulder alights from the vehicle. He swivels about as if surveying the field while the FX slowly rolls past him.

(*Note: An air-conditioned service van operating as a public utility vehicle)

He accosts the woman who barely has enough room to back off with other waiting commuters behind her.

Without warning, he PUNCHES the woman who flails backward to the people behind. Everyone freezes in stone-cold horror, including Freddie. Immediately, the thug scoops up the baby from the carriage.

He scampers off with the child. No one dares give pursuit except the mother, but he proves too fast for her.

He scoots over to the FX that's waiting around the bend and quickly hops inside. As soon as he and the "merchandise" were secured, the FX roars off.

EXT. NEIGHBORHOOD STREET - LATER

FREDDIE runs into one of their apartment neighbors. He swings the grocery bag behind his back.

                    MALE NEIGHBOR
          Where'd you come from?

                    FREDDIE
          Grocery.

The bag of milk-can swinging behind draws neighbor's attention.

                    MALE NEIGHBOR
          Hey, who's that for? You?
               (chuckles)
          What's the matter? Mommy's titties not
          good enough for you anymore?

                    FREDDIE
               (groping)
          Ha-ha. It's for my nephew, you dope.
          We're visiting my sister this Sunday.
          She just gave birth.

                    NEIGHBOR
               (chuckles)
          Really? I didn't know you had a nephew.
          Or a sister.

                    FREDDIE
          Well, you do now.

                              (hurries along)
                    Later, dude.

INT. THEIR APARTMENT - LATER

The TV volume is full blast.

FREDA is at the dining table, feeding the baby with mashed
banana. FREDDIE sits next to her, helping himself to their
lunch. The baby milk-can rests on a far corner of their table.
Judging from her horrified reaction, it seems he has brought her
up to speed about what went down at the supermarket.

                         FREDA
               Poor woman. And nobody helped? Where
               are those Baby Poos when you really need them?

He shrugs, takes a bite of the dried fried herring then chases
it with two spoonfuls of rice.

                         FREDA
               What would you do if that happened to you?

                         FREDDIE
               You mean if that guy punched me and took my kid?

                         FREDA
               Yeah?

                         FREDDIE
               I dunno.

                         FREDA
               So, you're just going to let that guy
               take your kid?

                         FREDDIE
               He's big. And there are others with him.

                         FREDA
               So? That's it?

He turns to the child. The baby is frowning at him.

ON TV -

The woman of the missing baby is again making her appeal to the
public. This time, she informs them that kid is wearing a
hospital-type bracelet tag that reads AM, for Anthony Mendez.
Then she flashes his picture on cam.

FREDDIE -

Stops cold and looks carefully at the tag flashed on TV

SMASH CUT: (FLASHBACK)

He picks up the tag that has peeled off from the laundry basket.

ON THE TAG -

The initials AM are inscribed on it.

BACK TO FREDDIE AND FREDA -

Their faces drop like a sack of potatoes. Their little bundle of
joy could be a ticking time bomb.

                         FREDDIE
               The tag. His tag. It says AM. Did you see that?

                         FREDA
               Yes.
                         (pause)
               But who knows? That could be just another kid
               with the same initials. That happens a lot,
               right?
                         (regaining her confidence)
               Besides, if that missing kid was our baby, don't
               you think, somebody would have already beaten us
               to him before he made it to our door?
               Think about it. Think about that baby you saw
               stolen in broad daylight. If this baby had just
               been left somewhere, a lot of people would have
               killed or get killed for it. And yet here he is.
               Safely with us. For once I can finally believe
               God performed a miracle for us.

                         FREDDIE
               But that baby. He looks just like him.

                         FREDA
              So? That happens a lot too. Haven't you heard of
              a doppelganger?

As the news shifts to the weather report, Freddie sinks in his
chair.

                         FREDDIE
              How are we going to keep our neighbors from
              hearing him? Seeing him? At some point…

She reaches for his hand and squeezes it.

                         FREDA
              Thirty days. Just like you promised. Just
              like we agreed. No one's going to see him.
              No one's going to hear him. I promise.

BEDROOM - THAT NIGHT

FREDDIE has zoned out and is snoring. FREDA is up on her feet
gently pressing a feeding bottle into the baby's mouth.

                         FREDA (VO)
                         (To baby)
              You know, if my hubby still had his job
              and our savings, I'd buy you.
                         (baby coos)
              Oh baby. I'm not sure I can give you up after
              thirty days.

Baby pulls back from the feeding bottle. His face lights up. He
smiles as if having read her thoughts. And then he cackles LOUD,
like that of a movie villain.

Before she could muffle his laughter, he rocks forward and
stretches his hand. He HAMMERS Freda's breast. She tries to
stifle a scream as she whisks away baby's hand off her chest.

                         FREDA
              No, baby. Don't do that. It's painful.

But baby reaches again for her breast and damps his palm on the
spot where nodule is located.

She freezes if she had just been anesthetized.

The baby's hand GLOWS like a magical wand as it caresses the spot.

                         FREDA (VO)
                         (stunned)
              What are you doing? What's happening?

Her mind swims. She lurches then nearly drops the baby. She hangs tight to the child then lands in bed.

FADE TO WHITE

THE FOLLOWING MORNING -

FREDA, in bed, wakes up disoriented, unsure how she even got here. She frets when she realizes -

The baby's not in her hands.

She whiplashes over to her side. To her relief, the baby is right there fast asleep on Freddie's vacated spot.

As she gazes at the child, she remembers something else.

Her hand cautiously roams her sick breast. Something's not right. She hauls out of bed and races to -

FRONT OF MIRROR

She slowly raises her shirt to find -

The cancerous nodule on her breast is GONE. Not a trace of it.

She whips around to face the child. He is smiling wide in his sleep.

DINING AREA - LATER

FREDDIE is lazily sipping his coffee. There is the usual egg and pan de sal by her spot waiting for her.

                         FREDDIE

O you're up. Pastor Roger just called. He
said he wants to present our case to the
elders to see how the church can help us.
For your treatment.

None of that sinks in. She is ashen white, her eyes hollow with
disbelief.

               FREDDIE
Are you okay? What's up with you?

               FREDA
Hon...
          (pause)
Could you watch the baby? Today?

               FREDDIE
What's the matter?

               FREDA
Nothing. I just need to see the doctor. Alone.

INT. DOCTOR'S CLINIC - LATER

FREDA'S oncologist is flabbergasted as she examines Freda's
breast.

The oncologist confirms what Freda had already seen this
morning.

The nodule has vanished from her breastscape.

               ONCOLOGIST
I don't believe it.

               FREDA
Is it gone?

Doctor retreats and motions to Freda to lower her shirt.

               DOCTOR
Yes. But I want to conduct
another test just to make sure.

               FREDA
What do you think happened, doc?

                              DOCTOR
                             (shrugs)
                    Lord knows. A miracle?

Freda smiles coyly, certain she won't need, much less pay for
another test.

INT. ROOM - SAME DAY

The baby is sucking on a feeding bottle, his eyes sparkling with
delight and holding his gaze at FREDDIE. Freddie gently taps his
thigh, lulling him to sleep. The baby whimpers then flashes a
wide smile.

LATER -

The baby is sleeping now. Freddie is on the edge of the bed,
back turned on him and plucking his guitar.

The baby snivels, then growls. Freddie whips around to check.
The baby looks asleep but is shifting restlessly as if having a
bad dream. Freddie leans in and taps his thighs. Baby is
mollified and resumes sleep.

As soon as he returns to his guitar playing, the child growls
again. He puts down his guitar and hovers over the baby, rubbing
his thighs.

BABY'S POV -

His eyes fixed on Freddie's scar.

                                        SMASH CUT:

SHIPPING LINER DOCK - FLASHBACK

A much younger FREDDIE is scaling up the side stairway of a
COMMERCIAL SEA LINER.

From above, something swoops down and SLAMS on his forehead.

BACK TO FREDDIE'S PRESENT -

The baby, wide awake now, flashes a sinister grin and then...BAWLS

FREDDIE freezes. He hears voices from the room of the adjacent
unit. Could they have heard the baby?

He scoops up the kid and fumbles on how best to hold him. It's
obvious he doesn't know how to hold a child in his arms. The kid
senses this and bawls some more. He is forced to gag him with
his palm.

                    FREDDIE
              Sssshhh!

He slings the baby on his shoulder and fumbles to switch on the
boom box. The kid is inconsolable now. He shushes the kid as if
to reprimand him.

Loud KNOCKING on his front door. Sweat beads dot his forehead.
He gingerly lowers the kid on the bed, his finger pressed
against his lips. He threatens the baby with a raised clenched
fist if he doesn't put a sock to his crying. He cranks up the
boom box volume another notch.

                    FREDDIE
              Ssshhh. Shut up, okay?

Baby cooperates and hushes. The knocking is followed by a female
voice calling out Freda's name. He recognizes it's their FEMALE
NEIGHBOR.

                    FREDDIE
              Stay there. And shut up, okay?

Baby snivels "yes."

DOWNSTAIRS - CONTINOUS

FREDDIE airs out his stress before opening the door.

                    FREDDIE
              Vangie. Hi.

                    FEMALE NEIGHBOR
              Hi Freddie. I didn't expect you to be home.
              Is Freda in?

                    FREDDIE
          She went to her doctor.

                    FEMALE NEIGHBOR
          You didn't go with her?

                    FREDDIE
          Ah, got some important stuff to take care
          off. She didn't want to bother me.
                    (Pause)
          What's this about?

                    FEMALE NEIGHBOR
          A mailman dropped this with us by accident.

She thrusts a letter envelope to him.

                    FREDDIE
          Thank you.

                    FEMALE NEIGHBOR
          Do you have a baby in the house? I thought
          I heard a baby crying. It's not mine.

                    FREDDIE
                    (Sarcastic chuckle)
          Baby? Ha-ha. You know we're the
          only babies in the house.

                    FEMALE NEIGHBOR
          Hmmm. I thought it was coming
          from your room.

                    FREDDIE
          Must be the radio. Or just missing my momma.
          Feeding time, you know?
                    (Chuckles)

                    FEMALE NEIGHBOR.
                    (Chuckles)
          Naughty. Well, won't take much of your time.
          Tell your mama I dropped by, you naughty baby.
                    (Pinches his arm)

ROOM - LATER IN THE DAY

FREDA, in her bra, pulls down her jeans and changes to her home shorts. FREDDIE sits silently by the edge of the bed, apparently flabbergasted with what she just said.

                    FREDDIE
          What? Are you sure?

She removes her bra and presses his hand to her breast.

                    FREDA
               Touch it.

His eyes pop in disbelief as his hand roams the spot that's now smooth as butter.

The baby whimpers then snivels. She quickly puts on a shirt, while he loads a CD-R in the boom box. "Nobody, Nobody but You" blasts out of the speakers.

                    FREDDIE
          How...?

She picks up the baby with his hand stretched to her. She affectionately presses his hand one her cheek.

                    FREDA
          When he touched my breast, his hand glowed
                    (pause)
          You know, like a bulb? I felt dizzy.
          Then I was out.
                    (pause)
          When I woke up, the lump was gone.

                    FREDDIE
          So...you're saying that baby did
          a John Coffey on you? You know, Green Mile?

                    FREDA
          Yeah. Something like that.
                    (pause)
          I know it sounds crazy. But
          maybe that's why God gave him to us.

                    FREDDIE
          An innocent baby. Performing miracles.
          Not even Jesus went that far.

                        (pause)
          I'm not sure…

                    FREDA
          Not sure about what? About the miracle?
          Or why he was given to us?

He swings around to check on the baby. Looks like "Nobody,
Nobody but You" has sent him back sleeping.

                    FREDDIE
          You really think he was sent here to do
          us some good?

                    FREDA
          Why would you doubt that?

The child bursts out laughing in his sleep, as if in mock
reaction to what Freddie said.

                    FREDA
          You still don't believe his coming to us is
          no accident? You're the one who always say
          there are no accidents. Everything happens
          according to God's plan.
                        (pause)
          Don't you suppose His plan is for us
          to keep this child?

He recoils at the suggestion. This is not what they agreed on.
The child cackles at him.

                    FREDDIE
          Oh no. No. Don't push it. Do you know
          what I went through today?

                    FREDA
          What?

                    FREDDIE
          Vangie was here this morning. To drop a letter.

                    FREDA
          A letter?

                    FREDDIE

That's not the point. I think it was just an
excuse to drop by. You know what she asked next?
If there was a baby in the house.
She heard a baby crying. In our room.
She was not imagining it. That little guy was
crying his lungs out for the whole world to hear.

                    FREDA
Oh gosh. That girl's a real snoop. And what did
you say?

                    FREDDIE
What else would I say? That it was the radio.
                    (pause)
You see a miracle, I see danger up ahead.
Next time that little sucker cries, it could be
Baby Poos banging on our door.

                    FREDA
You're overreacting. We've known them for year. I
don't think they'll do that…

                    FREDDIE
Don't be naïve. When it comes to money,
there is no family, no friends, and no
neighbors, no matter how friendly. The reward
is tempting enough for anyone to rat
you out.

                    FREDA
My, for somebody who reads the Bible a lot, you
really are a half-empty glass kindda guy.
                    (pause)
You see problems, I see blessings. And my
remission is just the beginning of it.

                    FREDDIE
Miracle or not, he's out of here after thirty
days. That was the deal, remember? No extensions.
Do you understand?

Freda and the baby trade giggles.

                    FREDDIE
Are we clear here?
                    (pause)

She plants a kiss on the baby, as if assuring him "Don't listen to daddy."

                         FREDA
               Yes, sir. All good, sir.

TV NEWS - ANOTHER NIGHT

Behind the newscaster is graphics for Super Lotto Draw.

                         NEWSCASTER
               Two hundred million, folks. Do you feel lucky?

DINING TABLE -

FREDDIE and FREDA react incredulously to the prize money
announcement. He returns to his dinner while she takes bites in
between feeding the baby. The next scene plays out as if they're
reading each other's thoughts.

                         FREDDIE (VO)
               Why can't it be that kind of miracle for us?
               Maybe it might change my mind about the kid
               if he lets us win that one.

                         FREDA (VO)
               Why don't you buy a ticket first? What?
               You expect this baby to magically pluck out
               a ticket in mid-air for you?

                         FREDDIE (VO)
               I would buy a ticket, if I had spare change.

                         FREDA (VO)
               Why don't you ask baby to give you a job so
               you can have that spare change?

They look at each other, stupefied, as if they had really read
each other's thoughts. Baby chuckles as if he had something to
do with their psychic exchange.

Freddie's cell rings upstairs. He's too lazy to go up and answer
it. Ringing stops but resumes after a minute. This time it rings
incessantly as if demanding to be answered.

                              FREDA
                    Don't you want to get that?

BEDROOM - CONTINUOUS

FREDDIE picks up the phone and checks the number on the LCD. He
doesn't recognize it but answers it anyway. He puts it on
speaker phone.

                              FREDDIE
                    Hello?

                              MALE CALLER (VO)
                    Hello? Who is this?

                              FREDDIE
                         (Regrets answering it)
                    Who are you? You're the one calling.

                              CALLER (VO)
                    Roland. Who's this?

                              FREDDIE
                    Roland who?

He hears disturbing noises on the other line - clashing,
clanging sounds as if someone was trashing the place. The
caller's voice trails off as he moves away from his piece.

                              CALLER (VO)
                    Who's there?

                              FREDDIE
                    Hello?

More things topple and crash on the other line. Then we hear a
pistol cocked.

                              CALLER (VO)
                    Oh shoot! No!!!

BANG! Caller screams.

                              FREDDIE
                    Hello?…

Line goes dead.

                         FREDDIE
                    Hello?!

He tries to call back. After several rings, he is told "The
subscriber cannot be reached."

DINING - CONTINUOUS

FREDDIE descends the steps, spooked. FREDA, gets up from her
plate and casts an inquiring glance at him.

                         FREDA
               What took you so long? Who was it?

He drops on his seat, still visibly stunned and not sure what to
make of it.

                         FREDDIE
                    No one. Probably some douche wanting
                    a *pasa load.

 (*Note: a modus where someone tricks a pre-paid subscriber to
share his load)

                         FREDA
               So, what took you so long?

                         FREDDIE
                    He was making all these strange noises.
                    Wouldn't answer.

The baby chuckles again, his eyes trained on Freddie as if
telling him he knows something.

ROOM - ANOTHER DAY

FREDDIE and FREDA are still asleep. It's way past their usual
waking hour. The baby is awake and cackling between them.

Freddie's cell rings. It is Freda not FREDDIE who gets roused.
Her hubby is sleeping like a log and snoring his blues away. She
gently nudges him.

                          FREDA
                    Hon, you're phone.

He wakes up, grumpy like anyone whose sleep has been
interrupted. He reaches for his phone underneath his pillow. The
number is again unknown. He is reluctant to take it. The ringing
dies.

He slides the phone back under his pillow. No sooner had he
returned to sleep when his cell rings again. Angrily he pulls it
out and finally takes the call.

                          FREDDIE
               Hello?
                    (suddenly mollified)
               Yes? Yes, speaking.
                    (rocks to a sitting position, excited)
               Yes! Of course. How's tomorrow?
                    (pause)
               Okay. I'll be there.

He ends the call then turns to a wondering Freda.

                          FREDA
               Who was that?

                          FREDDIE
               The girl who interviewed me. They want me
               to come back.

INT. OFFICE- ANOTHER DAY.

FREDDIE tapping his fingers sullenly on the desk. A female HR
SUPERVISOR sits behind it.

                          HR SUPERVISOR
               Actually, we had already chosen somebody.

                          FREDDIE
               Is that so? Why the change of heart?

                          HR SUPERVISOR
               Would you believe? We got a call

                              yesterday from his relatives saying he's dead.
                              Murdered.

                                        FREDDIE
                              Whoa. Who did you say he was?

                                        HR SUPERVISOR
                              Roland. Roland Garces.

                                        FREDDIE
                                        (Shocked; remembers name)
                               What happened?

                                        HR SUPERVISOR
                              Apparently, somebody broke into his
                              apartment and shot him.

                                                          SMASH CUT -

FLASHBACK -

FREDDIE, on his cell, listening to a pistol cocked on the other
line.

                                        CALLER (VO)
                                        (cont.)
                              Shoot! No!!

BANG!

BACK TO FREDDIE AND HR SUP -

                                        HR SUPERVISOR
                              Well, what can I say? Bad news for him.
                              Good news for you. Weird, huh?

                                        FREDDIE
                              I guess.

INT. MALL - OUTSIDE DONUT SHOP - LATER

FREDDIE is celebrating his hiring with a modest coffee and
donut. Suddenly -

Crowds disperse as a squad of BABY POLICE storm through. The
three in front have their arms locked around a cuffed MAN, about
Freddie's age. He is pleading that the baby is his. He is told
to shut his pie hole and argue his point when they reach
headquarters.

Baby in question is secured by one of the two Baby Poos behind
them.

FREDDIE fidgets and could barely bite his donut.

From that dispersed crowd, A WOMAN about Freda's age accosts
him. He recognizes her as Freda's friend.

                    FREDA'S FRIEND
          Freddie! I thought that was you.

                    FREDDIE
          Lydia?! I didn't know you were back.

                    FREDA'S FRIEND
          Yeah, about a year ago. But I'll be leaving
          again, in two months.
                    (her eyes seem to
                    examine him)
          How are you? How are things with you?

                    FREDDIE
          Great actually. Got a new job. Starting
          next week…

                    FREDA'S FRIEND
          Great to hear.
                    (pause)
          You've fully recovered I see.

                    FREDDIE
          Recovered? From what?

                    FREDA'S FRIEND
          Oh. Freda said you had cancer.
          That's the reason why she went home.
          That was her excuse.

He rides along not wanting her to catch a lie.

                    FREDDIE
          Oh…yes. Sorry, yeah.
                    (pause)
          Yes, I was diagnosed with cancer. But they
          caught it early. Freda rushed home thinking
          it was serious.

                    FREDA'S FRIEND
          Well, that's great to hear.
                    (pause)
          And Freda? How is she? Does she plan
          to work again?

                    FREDDIE
          Burning a hole in our couch. Stays home
          much of the time. She says she doesn't
          want to leave unless I go with her. I said
          good luck with that.

                    FREDA'S FRIEND
          I wonder if she heard about what happened to
          our friend, Marissa?

                    FREDDIE
          I'm not sure. What happened?

                    FREDA'S FRIEND
          She's in jail now for manslaughter. The baby
          she was looking after died. She was accused
          of negligence and who knows what else.

                    FREDDIE
          Wow!

                    FREDDA'S FRIEND
          Freda knows the baby. She was also
          his nanny. From what I heard, it was Marissa who
          took over her shift the night the baby died. I'm
          sure she'd be shocked to hear that.

                    FREDDIE
          Yeah…
                    (wondering what really happened)
          I'm sure.

INT. APARTMENT - LATER

FREDDIE silently digs into his plate. FREDA takes bites between
feeding the baby. TV is on.

                    FREDA
          So, what if you're a last minute replacement?
          The important thing is you have a job now.
          That's all that matters. Why should that make it
          less of you?
                    (Freddie shrugs continues
                     to eat)
          So, what happened to the guy they
          hired before you?

                    FREDDIE
                    (Shrugs; obviously reticent)
          They didn't say. And I didn't bother to ask.

He picks up the remote and surfs channels. He stops at a drama
series where the story unfolds in the nursery section of a
hospital. Something jogs his memory.

                    FREDDIE
          Hey, I ran into your friend. Lydia?

                    FREDA
          Lydia. From New Jersey? She's back too?
          What's up with her?

                    FREDDIE
          Well, she wanted to know if you've heard
          about your other friend over there. Marissa?
          She's doing time now.

                    FREDA
          Huh? For what?

                    FREDDIE
          Manslaughter. The baby she was looking after
          died and she was charged with negligence. Lydia
          said you knew the baby.

                    FREDA
          Knew the baby?

Her reaction says she does, but she tries to downplay it. She
sways the baby in her arms and then pretends to jog her memory.

                    FREDA
Oh gosh? Did she mean Jasper? How exactly
did she…?

                    FREDDIE
                    (Shrugs)
She didn't say much. I didn't ask much.

                    FREDA
Omigosh. I feel so bad for Marissa.

                    FREDDIE
Yeah. I'm sure. Then she told
me another story.

                    FREDA
About?

                    FREDDIE
About why you came home. You said it
was because I had cancer.

Silence. She pretends to be more interested in the TV drama
where a baby had to be rushed to surgery.

                    FREDDIE
Why would you say something like that?

                    FREDA
Look I was miserable there. I really wanted to
come home. If I said I was homesick you think the
hospital would let me get off my contract?

                    FREDDIE
But why didn't you tell me? Why did you have to
make up another story? It was a good thing Lydia
fired first. I would have asked why you were
suddenly retrenched.

                    FREDA
I'm sorry, okay. I made a mistake. I was
confused. I was just so lonely, I had to
get away from there.

                    FREDDIE (VO)
                    (returns to his plate
                    now almost empty)

                    Is that really it? Or is that another lie?

She touches the baby's bottom. The baby needs a diaper
replacement. She excuses herself and rushes him upstairs.

INT. WORSHIP HALL - ANOTHER DAY

Worship service has just concluded. FREDDIE walks out of the
venue alone when his PASTOR, his D-group leader, spots him and
rushes to greet him.

                         PASTOR
                    Freddie!

                         FREDDIE
                    Pastor.

                         PASTOR
                    It's been weeks since we last saw you.
                    Where's Fredda? How is she?

FLASHBACK - EARLIER

FREDDIE is busy getting ready for worship. FREDA is wiping poo
off the baby and replacing his diaper. He casts a reprimanding
stare at her. It's obvious she won't be joining him today.

                         FREDDIE
                    Tsk.Tsk. Now even your day with God is put
                    aside because of that kid.

                         FREDA
                    Oh God would understand. My body may not be
                    there. But my spirit is His and all my dirty
                    thoughts too.
                              (looks up as if talking to God)
                    Right, God? We're cool? Besides, I'm sure he
                    much prefers I send this baby to sleep than me
                    sleeping at His pastor's sermon.
                              (pause)
                    Right, baby?

Baby snickers at Freddie.

BACK TO WORSHIP HALL -

                    PASTOR
          I have spoken with the elders. They want to meet
          the two of you so you can give them an estimate
          of Freda's treatment. When can you be available?

                    FREDDIE
               (stunned)
          Oh? I wasn't expecting a quick reaction.

                    PASTOR
          I was surprised myself. But there you go.
          God's timing is always perfect. Now everything's
          up to you.

                    FREDDIE
          Ummm. Can I call you regarding that, Pastor?
               (groping)
          I just got a new job. I will be starting in
          a week.

                    PASTOR
          Wow! Isn't God amazing? That's a double cause
          for celebration, don't you think?

                    FREDDIE
          I guess so.

INT. BEDROOM - ANOTHER DAY

FREDDIE pulls down his shirt, getting ready for work. He is
garbed in typical IT work attire- sneakers, t-shirt, denim
pants. FREDA sits at the edge of the bed, looking after the
sleeping baby while also keeping watch on his husband's posture.
She brushes off dabs of baby powder from his shirt.

KNOCK downstairs.

                    VOICE DOWNSTAIRS (OC)
          Hello?! Anybody home?

Stunned silence. That doesn't sound like one of their neighbors.

                    FREDDIE
          I'll get it.

LIVING ROOM - CONTINUOUS

He opens the door to -

A MAN in a tie, with an ID that says NSO OFFICER. Behind him are
two BABY POLICE OFFICERS, strikingly daunting despite wanting to
appear congenial. Beads of sweat spring out of FREDDIE'S
forehead.

                    NSO OFFICER
          Good morning, sir. I'm from the NSO.
          I would just like to inform you of our new
          service. Do you have a new-born?

Freddie could almost feel his face melting like wax.

                    FREDDIE
          Ah… no. Everyone here knows we're childless.

                    NSO OFFICER
          Oh, I see. Sorry to hear that.
                    (pause)
          But hey, you can never tell.

                    FREDDIE
          So, what is this new service anyway?

                    NSO OFFICER
          Oh. I was about to say that If you have a
          New-born with no C.H.I.P. yet, you don't have to
          go all the way to our main office to do so. Now
          you can get it at your *barangay center.

(*Note: A local government unit center assigned to every
district. Barangay is also how a cluster of communities is
zonally categorized)

                    FREDDIE
          Thanks. But like I said, we have no kid.

                    NSO OFFICER
          How about you? Prospective parents
          can also get one for them.

                    FREDDIE
          Thanks. But what for? I think my wife's past
          that age of getting pregnant.

                    NSO OFFICER
          Who knows? Nothing is impossible. Especially
          these days.

                    FREDDIE
          Yeah. Right. See this scar on my forehead?
                    (pointing at it)
          That's God's sign that I won't ever need
          a C.H.I.P.

                    NSO OFFICER
          Why what happened to that?

                    FREDDIE
          Oh. Long story. And I can see you still have
          a long day ahead of you.

                    NSO OFFICER
          Okay, but what if you decided to adopt?
          That could still be in the cards, right? So why
          not get a CHIP now?

                    FREDDIE
          Ha-ha. Is Revillame or Baby Care giving you
          commissions for this?

A BABY'S WAILING from above sends the NSO Officer and the two
Baby Poops craning upwards to their bedroom window. Freddie
fidgets but tries hard not to show it.

                    FREDDIE
          I can assure you that's not ours.

True enough, the mother next door appears by the window upstairs
cradling her inconsolable infant. A relieved Freddie smiles at
the NSO officer. The uptight Baby Poos relax their guard as
well.

                    FREDDIE
          See? I told you so.

                    NSO OFFICER
          Thanks for your time. Have a good day sir.

As the men depart from their door, FREDA juts out of the window,
cradling the baby in her arms with her hand on his mouth to
muffle his cries.

INT. FREDDIE'S NEW OFFICE - SAME DAY.

HR Sup that interviewed him introduces FREDDIE to his new office
mates. Tepid hellos from most; some too engrossed in their work,
wave without even looking at him.

The intro tour ends, and he is turned over to his SUPERVISOR who
leads him to his assigned desk. It's totally cluttered and
messy.

                    SUPERVISOR
          My apologies for this mess. The one you
          replaced gave short notice of her resignation.
          She left without even clearing her
          desk. I trust you can manage?

Freddie shrugs "sure". His Supervisor leaves him so he can get
settled.

LATER-

His trash can is now teeming with his predecessor's abandoned
garbage. He opens the last unchecked drawer where mercifully
only a couple of pieces remained to be discarded. One is his
predecessor's family photo.

The other is an unmarked/unused Lotto ticket. He dumps both in
the trash can.

INT. APARTMENT - NIGHT

TV NEWS -

AM's MOTHER appealing to viewers.

                    AM'S MOTHER

                    I just want to say we're raising the reward to
                    three hundred thousand for any information
                    leading to my son's recovery.

The reward money draws FREDDIE'S full attention away from his
dinner. He casts a vicious albeit furtive glance at the baby in
Freda's arms before returning to his meal.

                         FREDDIE (VO)
                    Three hundred thousand. Wow.
                         (pause)
                    Mommy, are you sure you don't want to
                    cash in that baby yet?

FREDA shoots a glance at him as if she had read his mind.

                         FREDA (VO)
                    Cash? Is that all that matters to you?
                    No wonder God never gave us a child.
                    If He did, you might have already sold
                    him already to the Chinese.

He casts a hurt look at her as if he read her thoughts this
time. The next news item draws his attention again.

TV NEWS -

                         MALE ANCHOR
                    Brace yourself.Tonight's Super Lotto
                    draw is up to two hundred thirty million.

INT. FREDDIE'S OFFICE - ANOTHER DAY

FREDDIE is glued to his desktop.

His cell phone rings from inside his drawer. He tries hard to
ignore it. The ringing dies only to resume again after a minute.
This time it is relentless, demanding his immediate attention.

He caves in and whips it out of the drawer. He finds -

A Lotto card with a cluster of numbers already marked tucked
underneath it. He wonders if any of his colleagues had placed it
there by mistake.

                    FREDDIE
                 (waving the card)
          Did any of you guys leave this here?

His colleagues shake their heads, some without even looking at
him. He dumps the card in his trash bin.

His pesky cell phone continues to pest him. Finally, he checks.
It's FREDA calling. Suddenly, he feels guilty for not having
answered it right away. But when he does -

It's not FREDA'S voice but some boisterous laughter that begins
with that of a child's and gradually morphs to that of an
adult's giving him the creeps.

                    FREDDIE
          Freda? Freda!

The line dies. He rings up Freda's number. This time it's -

                    FREDA (VO)
          Dad?

                    FREDDIE
          Were you calling me?

                    FREDA (VO)
          Hmmm. No. Why?

                    FREDDIE
          Nothing. I just thought you were trying
          to call me.

                    FREDA (VO)
          No. Why? What's going on?

                    FREDDIE
          Nothing. Talk to you later. Got to get
          back to work.

He replaces his cell phone in his drawer.

No sooner had he returned to his work when Freda's ring tone
starts bugging him again.

He whips it out of the drawer and again finds -

Another Lotto card tucked underneath. What's going on here?

He examines the card – the same numbers from the card he disposed are again marked here – 3, 16, 17, 5, 10, and 2.

His cell phone pests him. He takes the call. Again, it is not Freda but a child's laughter that blasts in his ears. He wants to kill the call, but something holds him back.

He replaces the card in his drawer while the child's mischievous chuckles continue to assault his ear.

Laughter shifts to gloom as the child snivels and weeps.

He looks around; wanting to cry for help, but the strange force controlling him prevents him from opening his mouth.

The child cranks up the ear-splitting tear jerking. The voice leads him to slowly open his drawer. When he does, the weeping recedes.

The Lotto card glares at him. Grieving turns to guffaws and somehow he draws a clue from that.

He shuts the drawer and tests what he thinks is happening here. Immediately laughing shifts back to weeping. When he opens drawer, laughter resumes. Was this voice telling him something about the card? He picks it up.

FREDDIE'S POV –

The circle marks on the numbers glow like a lamp.

Delicious laughter on the other line.

INT. APARTMENT/THEIR ROOM – SAME DAY

The boom box is turned up enough to conceal the baby's inconsolable tears. FREDA tries to feed the baby but his head swivels away from the feeding bottle.

She damps her hand on the child's forehead. He is feverish. The child sensing this cranks up the tears, forcing her to dial up the volume some more. She picks up the baby and cradles her in

her arms. She rocks him to sleep but the baby is not in the mood
for this either.

                    FREDA (VO)
          Baby, what do you want? Please tell mommy
          cause I don't know what to do.

She sings along with the boom box and shakes him harder in
desperation. The child's weeping voice appears to be bouncing
but losing steam. His neck is swinging to and fro like a wrung
rag doll. Then his voice dies completely. She fears that by
shaking him too hard, she might have snapped his neck.

The child is still. No signs if he is still breathing. She
gently taps his cheeks with her finger. The child is not
responding.

                    FREDA (VO)
          Baby, no, please…I'm so sorry.

She taps his cheeks once more. This time, the baby coughs then
mumbles.

                    FREDA (VO)
               (Weeping but relieved)
          Oh, baby, baby. I'm so sorry.

EXT. LOTTO OUTLET KIOSK- SAME NIGHT

There is a long queue. The announcement board reminds bettors
that tonight's pot is 230 million big ones.

FREDDIE hands the filled-out card to the clerk.

His cell phone rings. It's Freda's number. Is it really her? He
takes the call anyway

                    FREDA (VO)
          Dad, are you on your way home?

INT. APARTMENT - LATER

FREDDIE arrives to find FREDA slumped on the couch, dampening
the baby's forehead with an ice bag.

The TV is on and cranked up loud.

                    FREDA
          Were you able to buy it?

He whips out a bottle of liquid paracetamol for infants from his
bag and places it on the dining table.

                    FREDDIE
          What happened?

                    FREDA
          He's been feverish since this afternoon.

He checks the time. He picks up the remote to change channels.

ON TV -

The Lotto draw is just about to start.

                    FREDA
          Why are we watching that?

He ignores her. The draw commences. The first number ball shoots
out of the dispenser. The TV HOST picks it up to read.

                    TV HOST
          The first number is 3.

He is hooked. She stares at him inquiringly.

                    FREDA
              Hon…?

                    FREDDIE
              Ssssh.

The succeeding number balls roll out - 16 followed by 17.

He pulls out his Lotto ticket from his bag. His eyes pop. So
far, he's gotten three numbers right.

                    FREDA
          You bought a ticket?

He ignores her, this time heavily invested on the outcome.

The next numbers roll out - 5, 10

One more to go. His jaw drops when the Host announces the last
number -

                              HOST
                    And finally, the last one - it's 2!
                    So, there you have it, folks.
                    Tonight's winning combination is
                    3, 16, 17, 5, 10, and 2. If that's yours,
                    then 230 million is yours to keep.

He drops on the couch stunned beyond belief.

                              FREDA
                    What? Did you win?

He passes the ticket to her, eyes locked on the TV. Upon seeing
the ticket, she launches a scream but he immediately hushes her.

                              HOST
                    And if anyone of you did win, please do
                    remember our less fortunate brothers by
                    donating a CHIP or two to them.

The baby erupts with delicious laughter. Freda damps her hand on
his forehead. The fever has cooled off and she hasn't even given
him the medicine yet.

EXT. FREDDIE'S NEIGHBORHOOD - ANOTHER DAY

A MOVING VAN pulls over across the street where the couple
lives.

A 16-year old BOY riding shotgun alights from the truck and
races over to the back of the truck.

From the same side of the truck, a fortysomething WOMAN alights
as well. She looks a lot younger than her age and could easily
be mistaken for the boy's older sister.

FREDDIE'S STREET - CONTINOUS

The boy shepherds a mountain bike while carrying a small box,
ahead of two movers, each one hoisting two big boxes each on
their shoulders.

They brush past the residents who don't pay them any mind.

Mother glances at the apartment row where Freddie and Freda
live.

INT. BANK - SAME DAY

FREDDIE is filling out a form

                    ACCOUNTS OFFICER
          Will this be a joint account, sir?

                    FREDDIE
          Yes. And make the signatories and/or.

INT. OFFICE - LATER

An ACCOUNTING CLERK drops by FREDDIE'S table with forms.

                    CLERK
          Freddie?

                    FREDDIE
          Uh-huh.

                    CLERK
          Could you fill this out, please? It's
          to update your records. You know? In case you
          have new dependents to declare.

He takes the form and quickly scans it.

FLASHBACK - ROOM

The baby is sound asleep and squeezed between them. Both of them
are in bed and still wide awake with excitement as if a whole
new future has opened up for them.

                    FREDDIE
          You're right. That kid might

have been heaven-sent after all.

                FREDA
Because of Lotto?

                FREDDIE
Yes. But here's the thing. Those
winning numbers? I didn't choose them.
It's as if somebody whispered them in my ears.

                FREDA
You mean like God whispered it to you?

SMASH CUT: OFFICE FLASHBACK

He's listening to the chilling laughter on his phone.

                FREDDIE (VO)
Yeah. Something like that.

BACK TO THEM -

                FREDA
See? God talks to you in a way you can
understand. Money.

Her arm drapes across his chest and caresses it.

                FREDA
So. Are you okay that the baby stays with us?
Mmmm a little bit longer? Who knows what else
God might whisper in your ear?

He mulls it over, still not sure that would be right.

BACK TO OFFICEFREDDIE -

ON THE FORM -

He hovers over the section regarding his number of dependents.

INT. APARTMENT - NIGHT

Empty cheap Chinese take-out packs litter their dinner table.
FREDA, on her feet, browses through the bank forms while lulling
the baby. FREDDIE slouches on his seat, eyes fixed on TV and
recovering from his heavy meal.

                    FREDA
          You think you can hold him while
          I fill this out?

As he reaches for the baby, he notices the kid seems transfixed
on his forehead scar.

The baby giggles, giving him the creeps. He reluctantly takes
the baby from her.

                    FREDA
          See, he likes you.

She lands on her chair and begins filling out the form.

He gingerly creates some space between him and the baby. The kid
snivels at this gesture and implores him instead to draw him
closer to him. She swivels to him and notices the gap between
him and the child.

                    FREDA
               (giggles)
          Don't worry. He's not going to piss all
          over you. He just did before we ate.

He relents and draws the baby tight to his chest. Baby
delightfully mumbles his approval.

                    FREDA
          See? Now you're BFFs

FLASHBACK - PIER

A very young FREDDIE climbs up the ship ramp. Trailing him is a
mother and her baby. In front of him is a tourist with a
professional camera slung around his neck and a tripod hoisted
on his shoulder that's perilously close to Freddie's face. The
tourist is trying to dodge a restless toddler jumping up and
down in front of him. The boy may be testing the ramp's strength
and endurance before collapsing and taking them all down. He

snaps at the kid's mother in English to rein in her pest. The
mother, embarrassed, tries to collar the boy but the brat breaks
free from her arm and jostles his way down the ramp. The
tourist, caught off-guard, backs off trying to avoid contact and
inadvertently hurls his tripod backward -

Smashing Freddie's forehead that immediately bleeds like a
geyser.

BACK TO FREDDIE AND BABY -

FREDDIE has warmed up to the kid, lulling him to sleep while he
drools on his chest. FREDA takes another pause from the form and
finds the whole scene between them endearing.

                    FREDA
          You do make a good daddy, you know?

ROOM - LATER

They're fast asleep now. The baby, asleep, lies between them
again.

Baby's eyes pop open. He snickers.

FREDDIE'S HAND, though he's asleep, crawls towards FREDA'S
behind and starts squeezing her tush.

Freda is roused and aroused by his horny hand. From the look on
her face, it seems like it's been a while since he pulled
something like that on her in the middle of the night.

Freda turns to face him only to find out his hand has been
conducting its affairs somnambulantly on her.

It doesn't matter. She reciprocates his sleepwalking hand by
reaching inside his shorts and seizing his pickle. It's only
then Freddie gets roused from sleep. They lock confounded
glances but indulge each other's urges.

LATER -

Only the baby remains on top of the now shaking bed. FREDA'S orgasmic moaning floats from the floor.

The baby is awakened but makes no noise of any sort so as not to disturb his copulating "adopters."

DINING ROOM - THE FOLLOWING DAY

FREDA is humming a tune while performing her chores.

EXT. THEIR STREET - SAME DAY

FREDDIE hops on the narrow pavement that could barely hold two pedestrians at a time to avoid motorcycles, owner jeeps and tricycles screeching in front and behind him. Once these transport modes are past him, he gets off the curb to avoid bumping into other pedestrians.

The new TEEN BOY on the block and on his bicycle, streaks towards him from an opposite direction.

Freddie's eyes meet the streaking boy head on, as if daring him "dude, I'm not getting out of your way, you get out of mine."

But the Teen Boy immediately shows him who's boss. He torpedoes straight for him without skipping a heartbeat. Freddie holds his ground but finally relents and hops on the curb in time to avoid getting swiped. The kid speeds on unapologetically. Freddie whips around and barks profanities at him. The Teen boy is undeterred, and he pedals on until he reaches the gate of their house.

Freddie's ire turns to one of surprise when the Teen boy enters the gates of the house.

INT. OFFICE - LATER

FREDDIE hangs by the panel divider of the ACCOUNTING CLERK'S cubicle. The Clerk looks over the blank section regarding dependents of his tax record form.

                         CLERK

                    So, you're planning to adopt?

                         FREDDIE
               Well, we're thinking about it.

                         CLERK
               As in buying a baby from Baby Care?

                         FREDDIE
               Isn't that expensive?

                         CLERK
               Uh-huh. Two hundred K a pup. Minimum, I hear.
               Sometimes it even goes as high as five hundred
               depending on the baby's gene. All high-end. The
               cheaper ones, you can go to the Chinese.
               But I'll be careful to buy from them. Yes,
               they're cheap. Their operation even looks legit,
               even their baby C.H.I.P. But…
                         (pause)
               You saw that news about those
               Americans who bought from them?

FLASHBACK –

INT. LICENSED DEALER'S OFFICE - DAY

A middle-aged American couple – missionary types – shifts
restlessly at the customer's lounge.

The shop's Chinese owner emerges from his office cradling in his
arms an indigenous new-born.

He parks near the couple and runs a Bio-Scanner across the
baby's eyes to reveal information about the baby.

ON THE BIO-SCANNER'S LCD:

"Registered to Mr.& Mrs. Henry Powell. NSO Reg. # 75012011.

The couple is pleased. The Chinese shakes their hands before
turning over their purchase to them.

EXT. PARK – ANOTHER DAY

The American couple is taking their newly purchased baby for a
stroll with the man pushing the stroller. They exchange smiles
with those passing by who couldn't resist stealing a glance at
their cute purchase.

They run into a couple of Baby Police. The Poos smile politely
at them which they promptly reciprocate. The Poos' attention
shifts to the baby in the stroller. The couple is about to move
on when one of the Baby Poos hoists his hand, prompting them not
to take another step. They oblige.

                         HUBBY
               Is anything the matter, officer?

                         BABY POLICE 5
               That baby. Yours?

                         WIFE
               Yes. We just adopted it.

                         BABY POLICE 5
               You mean you bought it?

                         WIFE
               Yes, we did.

                         BABY POLICE 5
               From Baby Care?

                         HUBBY
               No. But…

The Poos exchange smirks as if smelling blood.

                         BABY POLICE 4
               Can we check the baby?

                         HUBBY
               Of course.

Hubby picks up the child and hoists it. The Poo runs his Bio-
Scanner across the child's eyes.

The LCD flashes information different from what we saw earlier.
Instead it reads:

"Property of Ms. Samantha Choo - Registered Baby Care Property #653789.

                         BABY POLICE 4
          Are you Missus Choo?

                         WIFE
          Huh? No, I'm Betty Powell. This is my
          Husband, Hank.

                         BABY POLICE 5
          I'm sorry but this baby is registered
          to a Missus Choo.

                         HUBBY
          There must be some mistake. We checked with the
          seller. That baby is registered to us.

                         BABY POLICE 4
          Where did you buy this baby?

                         B. LALAKI
          From a licensed dealer. UR Baby. The owner
          scanned the child in front of us before turning
          him over. It said, "Registered to Mister and
          Missus Henry Powell". We saw it ourselves.

Meanwhile, kibitzers have swarmed them.

                         BABY POLICE 4
          I hate to break it to you, but I think
          you got duped by a Chinese bogey.

                         WIFE
          A what?

                         BABY POLICE 4
          A bogus dealer. There are many of those in
          Binondo.

                         HUBBY
          That's where we went.

                         BABY POLICE 5

That's where all those bastards are - legits, the
pirates all Chinese. You should have checked with
NSO first.

                    WIFE
But we checked out the dealer. They have a
license.

                    BABY POLICE 5
They can fake that too. And chances are, you
won't find that bastard when you go back there.
These Chinese a - -holes move around a lot. Makes
you wonder why the government is not coming down
hard on them.

                    HUBBY
So, what happens now?

                    BABY POLICE 4
You need to come with us.

                    BABY POLICE 5
And you'll have to leave your purchase with us.

                    WIFE
What? We paid good money for this.

                    BABY POLICE 5
Sorry ma'am. The law's the law.

                    HUBBY
And if we refuse?

                    BABY POLICE 4
Then we'll have to arrest you.

                    WIFE
                    (to hubby)
Honey?

                    HUBBY
Just do as they say. Give them the baby.

She reluctantly hands the baby to them in tears. One of the Poos
radios for back-up.

                    BABY POLICE 5

Central, copy? We have pick-up.
Request transport.

                    WIFE
Please officer. We didn't do anything wrong.

                    BABY POLICE 4
Yes. But we'll still need your statement.

BACK TO FREDDIE AND CLERK - END OF FLASHBACK

                    FREDDIE
Wow. Bummer.

                    CLERK
Yeah. Bummer.

                    FREDDIE
Okay. But what if…what if someone, let's say
left a kid by your door, no C.H.I.P., no nothing.

                    CLERK
You mean like a stork dropped it at your
doorstep. Dude, are you for real?
Nobody's dumb enough to leave precious
merchandise lying around.

                    FREDDIE
Yeah, I know, I know. I was just thinking…

                    CLERK
But for the sake of discussion, let's say someone
was stupid enough to leave a baby with you,
you'll need a good lawyer to fix that. The thing
is, the law requires that the Infant
Crime Unit takes temporary custody of that baby
while your case is pending in court. If in the
course of the investigation, it shows that the
abandoned kid has a C.H.I.P. and is proven
stolen, your attorney will now have to prove that
you were not in cahoots with anyone when you got
that baby. The cost of those legal proceedings
alone could buy you two Baby Care babies.

INT. INFANT CRIME UNIT LAB - DAY (FLASHBACK)

A huge room filled with cribs of babies confiscated by the Baby Police. They have no tags to them and it's likely they have no C.H.I.P. either.

A Baby Poo lowers another confiscated baby in a crib. A closer look reveals the baby looks very much like the AM kid under Freddie and Freda's care. The initials on his tag confirms it too - AM. The Baby Poo runs a Bio-Scanner across the baby's eyes. The baby has no C.H.I.P.

                    CLERK (VO)
          So, if you're getting a stray, you better
          pray that kid has no C.H.I.P. Abandoned or not,
          you have a higher chance of keeping that pup.
          That is if the Baby Poos don't get interested in
          it first. You see, things could easily get
          complicated if the baby is good looking.

The Baby Poo removes the tag from the C.H.I.P.-less baby and transfers it to an indigenous baby.

                    CLERK (VO)
          They'll switch the baby with one that's not so
          good- looking then they'll insist it's the baby
          you left with them. Of course, you can easily
          file a complaint but that will take
          time, more money, lots and lots of it, and in the
          end the courts could even favor the Poos.

BACK TO FREDDIE AND CLERK -

                    CLERK
          Damn bloody, if you ask me. So, you still
          want to adopt?

INT. APARTMENT/ROOM - ANOTHER DAY

Boom box drowns the hungry baby's boisterous clamoring for feeding.

DINING - CONTINOUS

FREDA is distraught to find out they have run out of milk.

ROOM - LATER

She lands on the bed and bends her body to the still
inconsolable baby.

                        FREDA
               Baby, I'm so sorry. We've run out of milk.
                    (pause)
               Can I leave you so I can buy some?

The baby wails in protest. She wonders if the volume is loud
enough to mask the apoplectic infant. She picks him up, rocks
him in her arms to hush him, but it doesn't work. She rocks him
further, oblivious that she's been shaking him way too hard
again. The baby stops crying but not reassuringly.

                        FREDA
               Baby? Baby?

After another beat of nerve-tingling silence, the baby snivels
to assure her he's okay.

                        FREDA
               What do we do? Please.

The child moans as if trying to communicate his suggestion.

                        FREDA
               You know I would take you if I
               could, right?

The child's mood shifts from glum to glee as if approving the
suggestion.

                        FREDA (VO)
               Huh? No? You can't be serious.

POV - CLOSET - LATER

Her arm stretches for the top of the cabinet. She pulls down a
big gym bag.

GARFIELD PIGGY BANK - LATER

Turned upside down, lid opened. She fishes out a couple of
hundred bills plus some loose change

BED - CONTINUOUS

She tries to fit the baby inside the gym bag. The bag
accommodates the child just fine.

The baby giggles delightfully.

                    FREDA
          Baby, please behave, okay?

Then she zips him up.

EXT. APARTMENT/COMMON AREA WALKWAY - LATER

A NEIGHBOR pops out of the house and jumps on her as she is
passing through.

                    FREDA
                    (rattled)
          Vangie?!

                    NEIGHBOR
          Hey! What's up with you, girl? When was the last
          time you got out? You've been holed up in the
          house too long? Planning to join the convent?

                    FREDA
          Me? Convent? You know if they're recruiting
          horny nuns now?

                    NEIGHBOR
          Ha-ha. Is that why your radio is loud
          all the time? So, you and Freddie can hide
          your loud Aaaaah-men?
                    (Makes Amen sound lusty)

They trade laughs.
                    FREDA
          You naughty bitch. I'll leave you with
          your dirty thoughts.

                         NEIGHBOR
              What's with the bag? Where are you headed?

                         FREDA
              Ummmm. Gym?

She says bye and hurries on. She hasn't gone far when the bag
wiggles. She nervously wheels about to check if the neighbor had
seen it. Good thing she has returned inside her unit.

EXT. APARTMENT GATE - CONTINOUS

As she thrusts out of the gate doors, her bag ahead of her, she
notices -

HOUSE ACROSS THEIR STREET - CONTINUOUS

The WOMAN and her TEEN SON are eyeing her behind their gate.

Her bag wiggles again. She forces a smile while keeping the
wiggling bag away from their probing eyes then promptly shuffles
off.

INT. GROCERY - LATER

FREDA hurries past the main entrance and is about to enter the
shopping area when -

                         MALE SECURITY GUARD
              Ma'am, excuse me. You can't bring that
              bag inside.

                         FREDA
              Oh? But I've got important stuff inside.

                         MALE SECURITY GUARD
              I'm sorry. But you're going to have to leave
              that here.

She reluctantly hands the bag to the Check-In Counter Boy. The
bag proves heaves for the gawky boy as he hauls it off the
counter. He slams the bag on the floor to FREDA'S horror.

                         FREDA

                    Oh gosh! You jerk! I got
                    breakables in there. Give it back!

The Counter Boy obliges and shuttles it back on the counter. She
drops her ear on the bag while her hands roam around it to
inspect. There is no sound or movement coming inside. Fear and
worry grip her. Is the baby okay? Should she leave now? But what
if he cries for his food?

She turns to the flustered guard.

                         FREDA
                    You moron! That's why I didn't want to
                    leave this with you. If something happens,
                    who are you going to blame, huh? The customer?

                         SECURITY GUARD
                    I'm so sorry. Did he damage anything?

                         FREDA
                    Fortunately for you morons, there's none.
                    Now, should I still leave this with you? After
                    what that jerk-o did?

                         SECURITY GUARD
                         (reluctant but finally relents)
                    It's okay. Go. Take the bag with you.

She immediately yanks the bag off the counter and hurriedly
walks to the shopping area. The bag wiggles to assure her
everything is okay. She looks back. The security guard and the
counter boy are now attending to another customer.

CASHIER - LATER

FREDA lands a medium can of powdered milk and a bag of
disposable diapers on the counter.

As the cashier registers the items, her attention is yanked
outside -

EXT. GROCERY - CONTINUOUS

Two BABY POLICE stop a couple of marginalized women, in their
thirties and bearing a new-born, for questioning and inspection.

The Bio-Scanner confirms that the women are legit owners of
their baby. The dismayed and unbelieving Baby Poos let them go.

BACK TO CASHIER -

The distraction makes FREDA oblivious to the CASHIER's queries -

                    CASHIER
          Ma'am…Excuse me, ma'am, how would
          you like to pay for this?

                    FREDA
          I'm sorry. How much is it?

                    CASHIER
          One thousand five hundred.

She pulls out her purse from her other bag and lands the cash on
the counter. She's a few pesos short. She fishes out her coins
to meet the balance. She barely has enough for a ride home.

EXT. STREET JUNCTION - LATER

FREDA joins the pedestrians cramping the island junction as they
wait to cross. The blinking red traffic light signals one
hundred sixty-five seconds before they can do so. She is bumping
elbows with the marginalized mothers who passed inspection by
the Baby Police earlier. They're trying to pacify their crying
baby.

Behind them, the Baby Poos continue their round of inspection,
stopping other shabby looking women with infants. Like the two
earlier, these mothers likewise pass the test and are
reluctantly released. They glance at the other pedestrians with
children standing behind those on the island.

Freda's bag wiggles just as the Baby Poos are coming their way.
Boisterous laughter, like that of an adult's, bursts out from
inside the bag. The people next to her and around her cast
inquiring glances at each other, wondering where that raucous
laughter is coming from. Is that from your cell phone or what?

The frozen Freda could almost feel her feet melting. She's
desperate to unzip the bag so she could suppress the manic

laughter coming from it. Still 50 seconds to go before she can cross to the other side. The Baby Poos are fast approaching.

She hops off the island and slithers her way through the parked cars back to the supermarket. The Poos are now circling those around the island.

By the time she reaches supermarket entrance, the light turns green for the island pedestrians. The Poos back off from the crossers but linger near the island. There's no way she can outrace them. Now, they're shifting their attention where she's standing. Her bag is not just laughing but wiggling too.

She circles the parking lot and slithers her way to the taxi bay stationed a few feet away from the island junction. There are no cabs available at the moment. She moves out of the bay and gets on the main road trying to hail a passing cab, even as her mind races to figure how she'll pay for this fare.

A cab streaks past and pulls up a few feet away from her. She dashes for it, but a millennial couple beats her to it. She slams the hood of the departing cab in rage. She turns to the island and sees the Poos have moved away from it and scanning the people, particularly with babies, going in or coming out of the supermarket.

The traffic light has again flashed green for the pedestrians crowding the island. She rushes to join the moving crowd, but before she can hit the pedestrian lane, the light again turns red forcing her to hop on the island. New pedestrians soon join her; some with babies in tow. She moseys over to the edge of the island, as the Baby Poos are now accosting this fresh batch of waiting pedestrians with babies. Her bag is now quiet and still as if cooperating with her tense moment.

An OLD GAY MAN hops on the island and jostles his way to move ahead of the pack. He is proudly carrying a blonde baby. The others cast furtive yet suspicious glances at him, including Freda and the Poos, who skip a couple of straight couples so they can go straight for the gay guy.

                    BABY POO 1
          Yours?

                    OLD GAY MAN
          Yes. I bought it.

                         BABY POO 2
                      Mind if we check?

Baby Poo 2 immediately runs the scanner on the blonde baby's
eyes and then Gay Man without waiting for his permission.

The Scanner blinks legit.

                         OLD GAY MAN
                      Satisfied? Officers?

Freda's bag wiggles again just as the light turns green. One of
the preying Baby Poos caught it but is not sure what he saw as
the Gay Man's shoulders were shielding Freda.

Freda rushes ahead of the crowd, scuttling towards a waiting
passenger jeepney.

                        BABY POO 1 (OS)
                       You! Stop there.

Busted? She wheels around slowly only to find the Baby Poo's
hand on the shoulder of another shabby looking mother with a
baby behind her. She resumes her dash for the passenger jeepney
and hops on.

INT. APARTMENT/ROOM- LATER

FREDA is now feeding the baby.

                         FREDA (VO)
               You naughty baby. I thought you were going
               to get us caught.

The child moans as if assuring her that was not his intention at
all. She brushes her cheek against his forehead lovingly.

                         FREDA (VO)
                  Please don't do that again, huh?

She drops on the edge of the bed, her body almost wilting from
the scary episode earlier.

EXT. THEIR HOME STREET- NIGHT

FREDDIE runs into other neighbors not from their apartment. They
exchange pleasantries.

A WOMAN calls out to him from across the street. He follows the
voice and finds -

That WOMAN who had just moved in standing from behind the gate
of her single detached home. He approaches her though he can
barely make out who she is as the faint streetlight and shadows
obscure her face.

                         WOMAN
               Don't you remember me?

                         FREDDIE
                         (Takes a harder look)
               Angela?

                         ANGELA
               How have you been?

He fidgets. This doesn't seem like a pleasant reunion for him.

                         FREDDIE
               Good. So, you live here now?

                         ANGELA
               I think I saw your wife this morning. With a big
               bag. She was in a hurry to leave.

                         FREDDIE
               Oh?

                         ANGELA
               She's pretty. What's her name?

                         FREDDIE
               Freda.

                         ANGELA
                         (nods)
               Freda. And you're Freddie. How lovely. Like split
               halves of a chamber pot
                         (He smiles, trying to
                         make light of it)
               Do you have matching shirts with
               your names on it?

                    FREDDIE
               (nods but hardly amused)
          Coffee mugs with our names on it.

                    ANGELA
          That's really sweet. Was that your idea or hers?
          And are your names engraved in a heart?

He nods at what is obviously a taunt then slowly backs away from
the gate.

                    FREDDIE
          Gotta go. She might be waiting for me.
               (pause)
          It was nice seeing you. Welcome to
          the neighborhood.

                    ANGELA
          Do you wanna know his name?

                    FREDDIE
               (stops)
          Whose name?

The TEEN BOY who nearly ran him over blasts out of the house's
screen door to join them. He and Freddie exchange nasty looks.

Freddie notices something else - the boy does bear some
resemblance to him.

                    TEEN BOY
          Aren't we eating yet?
               (His loathsome eyes not
               leaving Freddie)

                    ANGELA
               (Her eyes stay
               on Freddie as well)
          Get inside. I'll follow.

                    TEEN BOY
          I'm hungry. Who's that you're
          flirting with now?

                    ANGELA
          Get inside before I slap that cute cheek

of yours red.

The Teen Boy wheels about then grudgingly walks back inside the house.

                    ANGELA
          My apologies for his rudeness. He could be a
          bit insensitive, you know? I think he got it
          from his father.

                    FREDDIE
          Your boy?

                    ANGELA
                    (nods)
          AJ. Alfredo Juan, I named him after his dad.

The name spooks Freddie. He realizes what's going on but tries to play it down.

The Teen Boy makes raucous noises inside demanding dinner.

                    FREDDIE
          So…where's his dad?

                    ANGELA
          Came and went like a fart in the wind.

                    FREDDIE
          Uh-huh.
                    (pause)
          Why did you name him after him?

                    ANGELA
          To remind me of my stupidity. For believing a
          man's heart instead of his wanker.

                    FREDDIE
          Look, Angela...

                    ANGELA
          Do you still remember that day?

                              SMASH CUT -

ON HIS WINNING LOTTO CARD -

The rings circling the numbers 3, 16 and 17 light up.

                         ANGELA (VO)
               March 16. Seventeen years ago, to be exact.

FLASHBACK - MAGELLAN'S CROSS

SUPER: *17 Years Ago - Cebu*

A young FREDDE and ANGELA are seated on a park bench. She is
crying. He lands his hand on her shoulder to comfort her.

                         FREDDIE
               Don't worry. We can fix this.

                         ANGELA
               My father's going to kick me out of the
               house if he finds out I'm….
                         (more sobs)

                         FREDDIE
               Don't worry. That's not going to happen.

                         ANGELA
               You mean you're going to marry me?

He recoils at the suggestion; takes a deep breath.

                         FREDDIE
               You know I just got this job, right? I'm
               not even sure how I can support both of us
               with my salary.

                         ANGELA
               So, what's your plan then?

                         FREDDIE
               I know a clinic. They say it's safe.
               And it's cheap. I can manage that.

Horror builds up on her face when she realizes what he's
suggesting.

                         ANGELA
               Wait. You want me to drop this baby?

                        FREDDIE
Think about it. If we have that baby, what
happens? Sure, we can move in together but how
are we going to live?
                (pause)
Look, I want to have a life with you. And a
child. But not now. Help me save up for it first.
Believe me, dropping that child is our best
option. When we're finally married, we can easily
have another one. Or two.

                        ANGELA
I'm not sure. I'm afraid.

                        FREDDIE
Don't worry. I'll go with you.
                (holds Angela's hand)
Think about it. We do this thing, we can
start fresh. I work, I save, and you can finish
college. And if we both have jobs, then we can
have the life we want.
                (pause)
What do you say?

                        ANGELA
Okay. Let's do this. But don't leave me please.

                        FREDDIE
Promise. I won't.

BACK TO PRESENT FREDDIE AND ANGELA -

                        ANGELA
                (shakes head in dismay)
But you never showed up at that clinic.
I thought you simply forgot. So, I didn't
go through with it.
                (pause)
Days later I found out you had gone
back to Manila. That was your plan all along.
Leave the money for my abortion then
leave me completely.

                        FREDDIE
Angela…look, I panicked...

ANGELA
I was forced to leave home and stay with my
cousins. I thought my life was over. But when
AJ was born, my father found it in his heart to
forgive me. And he took me back home so I
could resume my studies.

FREDDIE
I'm truly sorry. I screwed up.
            (glances at his watch)
I need to go. Look, why don't we continue
this talk some other time, okay? Good night.

ANGELA
Yes. There you go running again as always.

FREDDIE
Angela…

ANGELA
You think my being here was just coincidence?
            (pause)
I know everything that has happened to
you since that time.
            (pause)
And I know there's something
you're hiding right now.

FREDDIE
What are you saying?

ANGELA
I know about the baby, idiot. The one your
wife snuck out of the house in a gym
bag this morning? Which makes you think…
            (pause)
Why would she keep that poor thing inside?
Because it's not hers and it's certainly not
yours.

Sweat rushes out all over him like a stream. Fortunately, nobody
has caught any of her last revelations. Not even the punks from
squatter areas busting their moves on makeshift skateboards.

ANGELA
Don't worry. I'm not going to report you

to the Baby Police. Not yet anyway.

            FREDDIE
So, what is this really about? Money? Payment for
my stupidity?

            ANGELA
Yes. It's about money.

            FREDDIE
Ha. You're timing really sucks. I just got a job
after being jobless for two years. My savings all
used up, more so when my wife got cancer.

            ANGELA
Wow. You really take me for stupid, do you?
Like I said I know everything about you –
including the 230 million you just won.

            FREDDIE
What?! How…

            ANGELA
Look. I'm not asking a lot. I just want half as
back pay. That's for raising your kid alone. It's
reasonable, don't you think?

            FREDDIE
Look, it's not going to be that easy. What will I
tell my wife? I can't do that.

            ANGELA
You can and you will. And you have until the end
of the month to do it. That's when the grace
period to keep the baby ends. After that, tsk,
tsk. Told you I know everything.

            FREDDIE
Angie, please…be reasonable.

            ANGELA
And don't get funny ideas this time.
Whatever s--t you're planning again to rip me
off, you won't get away. Somehow, some way,
whatever you do, I promise you I'm going to
get half of that money.

AJ shows up at the screen door.

> AJ
> Ma...should I go fix your room for you
> two? Why don't you just bring that
> dope-s--t inside and get on with it? And
> where's dinner?

> ANGELA
> In a minute you dip-s--t!

She backs of from the gate.

> ANGELA
> Remember. My money. End of the month.
> Good night.

INT. APARTMENT - LATER

FREDDIE arrives to find the can of milk and pack of diapers on
the dining table. So, it's true Freda had gone out this morning.

BEDROOM - CONTINUOUS

FREDA, lying beside the baby, gingerly pulls away the feeding
bottle from his lips. The baby is fast asleep. She's too wrecked
to even get up when FREDDIE appears and pauses by the door.

> FREDDIE
> Did you go out this morning?

> FREDA
> (rocks up)
> Who told you?

> FREDDIE
> So, you did go out?

> FREDA
> I had to. Baby's out of milk.

> FREDDIE
> And you brought the kid with you?

> FREDA

Who told you?

He switches on the boom box.

                    FREDA
          Keep it down. He just slept.
                    (pause)
          Who told you?

                    FREDDIE
          Who cares? Somebody saw you, that's
          the point. Gosh. What were you thinking?

                    FREDA
          If I didn't go out, he'd be hungry and crying
          the whole day. Loud. What do you think
          would happen, huh?
                    (pause)
          Who told you I was out?

                    FREDDIE
          Forget about it.

                    FREDA
          No, I need to know. If we're in trouble
          I need to know who squealed.

                    FREDDIE
          One of our neighbors saw you with a bag.

                    FREDA
          Vangie? She didn't suspect anything.

                    FREDDIE
          No, not from the apartment. It was Joe. I think
          he was looking out the window and saw you
          with that big bag. He wondered where you were
          headed.

                    FREDA
          Hon, I swear. I was careful. If I wasn't
          and got caught, you think I'd be here
          right now?

The baby chuckles in his sleep.

                    FREDDIE

                    Okay, okay. Forget it. Just don't
                    do that again.

EXT. THEIR STREET - NEXT DAY

FREDDIE thrusts out of their apartment gate, running late for
work. He finds -

ANGELA and AJ, standing behind their gate, keeping a close eye
on him. AJ smirks at him.

Freddie ignores them both and sprints off.

LATER -

Before he reaches their street's entrance, perpendicular to the
main thoroughfare, he feels somebody tailing him.

He whips around to find -

AJ slowly wheeling behind him on his bike. He stops. The boy
stops as well.

                         FREDDIE
                    What do you want?

                         AJ
                    Nothing. Just following mommy's orders.
                    Just making sure you don't leave us again,
                    douche.

Freddie walks up to him, his fists all balled up ready to clean
the boy's mouth with it.

                         FREDDIE
                    You want to report a bleeding nose to mommy?

                         AJ
                    I see now. She's right. You're a world-class
                    asshole!

That sent his fist flying. AJ backs off in time to dodge his
knuckle sandwich then speeds off laughing. AJ'S laughter sends
him chills that stop him from pursuing him.

It's the same kind of laugh he heard that day he placed his bet.

AJ, back on him, flips the bird to wave him goodbye.

EXT. BUILDING LOBBY - LATER

A svelte real estate AGENT stops FREDDIE on his tracks and hands
him a flyer. He takes it, not sure why he did besides checking
out the pretty thing. He glosses over it.

                    AGENT
          We have an open house this Sunday, sir. There
          are already a few units up for you to see.
                    (pause)
          I'm Annette by the way. If you're interested, you
          can call me. My number is there at the bottom.
                    (pointing to flyer)

He nods, thanks her and races to the elevator.

INT. OFFICE LOBBY - LATER

ANNETTE the agent shows him the map of the housing project. The
units sold have been yellow marked. She points the other lot
units still up for grabs in another phase.

                    AGENT
          These are the ones left. A bit far from the
          gate, yes. The ones closest have sold out.

                    FREDDIE
          Are there houses here already?

                    AGENT
          Yes. They're among the last batch to be built.

                    FREDDIE
          How soon can we move in if ever?

                    AGENT
          Well, sir, if you're ready to make a down
          payment now, we can get the papers started.

                    FREDDIE
          Wait here. I'll get my check.

INT. APARTMENT/ROOM - SAME DAY

Loud knocking downstairs alarms FREDA. She is reluctant to
answer it. But the knocking persists. The baby is awake and
feeding.

                    FREDA
          Baby, I need to get that. Can I leave you
          for a second?

She gingerly pulls out the bottle from his lips. Baby looks at
her and smiles.

                    FREDA
          I won't be gone long. Please be quiet?

DOWNSTAIRS/ DOOR- CONTINUOUS

Her door opens to a corpulent woman, mid-fifties to early 60s.
She is decently garbed. Her fingers and neck are sparkling with
jewelry; hard to tell whether fake or not. Grouse and
condescension hang on her crumpled face like any typical cranky
senior.

                    OLD WOMAN
          Are you Freda Mangahis?

                    FREDA
          Yes. And you are?

                    OLD WOMAN
          Amelita Boncayao. Marissa's mom. You still
          remember her, do you?

                    FREDA
          Of course, Marissa. How is she?
                    (pause)
          And what is this about?

                    OLD WOMAN
          May I come in?

LIVING ROOM - LATER

FREDA is a beehive of activity while keeping a tense ear
upstairs. Her unexpected visitor quietly notices this.

                    OLD WOMAN
          Is there something you need to do upstairs?

                    FREDA
          Ah no. That can wait.
          Can I offer you coffee?

                    OLD WOMAN
          Don't bother I won't take long.
                    (pause)
          Could you join me here, please?

She obliges and lands next to her. They exchange awkward
glances.

                    FREDA
          Anything you want to tell me?

                    OLD WOMAN
          You've heard about what happened to
          my daughter, do you?

                    FREDA
          Actually, a friend of mine told me about it.
          I couldn't believe it. Sad.

                    OLD WOMAN
          Yes, it's really sad considering she was
          innocent of the charges.

                    FREDA
          How so? Sorry, I never really knew what
          Happened, how she landed in jail.

                    OLD WOMAN
          The baby she was to babysit? He was
          already dead even before her shift started.

                    FREDA
          Is that so? How did that happen?

                    OLD WOMAN

You really wanna know? She wrote to me,
you see? From jail. She said you were the last
one to see that baby alive. You were in charge
before she took over for you.

> FREDA
Is she accusing me that I was the one who killed
the baby? I swear when I left the baby that
night, he was asleep. That's what I told
Marissa when she came in. She knows as much that
the slightest sound could wake him up, so she
didn't bother to check on him.

> OLD WOMAN
Unfortunately, my daughter took your word for it.
> (pause)
That was her mistake. She didn't even bother
checking his diaper because according to her,
you just changed him before she came.
She was relieved there was not much to do
because the baby was quiet as a mouse by the
time his parents came home. That was their
mistake too. They didn't bother to check on their
own baby.
> (sobbing now)
It was only the following day when they saw the
baby was not breathing anymore. And because
Marissa was the last one near him, they thought
she had something to do with it.

> FREDA
Like I said that baby was alive and fast asleep
when I left. That's what happened.

> OLD WOMAN
So, you're keeping that story.
> (pause)
Will you tell the same thing to God
when he appears to us now?

INT. ROOM- FLASHBACK

SUPER: *New Jersey - May 8TH, Two Years Ago*

FREDA is trying to appease the Caucasian baby in her care. He's
been crying for some time now and she's done everything to hush

him but to no avail. Her patience is drained. She shakes the
child in desperation.

                    FREDA
          Jasper, stop. Please.

The baby wails louder. She shakes him harder, perhaps more
intense this time like shaking a tree for its fruit to fall.

Shortly after, the baby finally relents to her and hushes.

He is awfully still and not breathing.

                    FREDA
          Jasper? Jasper?
               (panics)
          Jasper, no. Please. Wake up.

She shakes him again, hoping to rouse him this time. But the
child is now stiff as a doll. She lands on a chair, distraught,
not sure what to do next.

Then, she lands him in his crib and pulls his blanket over to
him. He could fool anybody peering in that he's only sleeping.

She kisses the baby's cold cheek. Her tears dampen his face. She
pulls out her hanky - the very same one she dumped with AJ's
wrappings in their laundry basket - to wipe his face.

The doorbell rings. Before answering it, she makes sure the baby
appears like he's only sleeping.

                    FREDA
          I'm sorry, baby. Bye.

We stay with the baby while she answers the door. It's MARISSA.
We can only hear their voices wafting from the living room.

                    MARISSA (OC)
          Hi girl!

                    FREDA (OC)
          Ssssshhh. He's sleeping.

SMASH CUT - LOTTO CARD

The encircled numbers 5, 10, 2 on Freddie's winning card light
up. Now we know why these numbers were predetermined. This
bunch represents the date of Freda's own transgression.

                    OLD WOMAN (VO)
          I believe two days after that night, you suddenly
          went back home. You told the hospital you were
          working for that you had an emergency.

BACK TO FREDA AND THE OLD LADY -

                    FREDA
          Yes. That's true. My husband was sick and he
          needed me. He had cancer.

                    OLD WOMAN
          Is that so?

Cries erupt from upstairs. Freda gets up and races for the
stairs

                    FREDA
          Excuse me. My baby needs me.

                    OLD WOMAN
          Your baby?

                    FREDA
          Yes.

                    OLD WOMAN
          Are you sure it's yours?

The baby hushes as if sensing a volatile situation.

                    FREDA
          Ma'am, I still have a lot to do. Unless there's
          something else, maybe it's best you leave now.

                    OLD LADY
          Your child, huh? Are you prepared to say the
          same thing to the Baby Police?
                    (Freda is stunned)
          I thought so.

                    FREDA

What do you want? Money?
You came to the wrong house. My US savings,
all that, gone. We have nothing to
give you.

                    OLD LADY
Really? That two hundred thirty million
gone too?
                    (pause)
You know? Lotto?

                    FREDA
How do you know all this?
Are you really Marissa's mom?

                    OLD LADY
Child, what's important is you know
that I know everything about you.
                    (pause)
Here's what I really want. I want half of that.
And you have until the end of the month to
deliver it. If not…
                    (whistles her doom)
I have a son working for the Infant Crime Unit.
Well you know where this goes if you don't pay.

                    FREDA
Look, even if I want to, my husband controls the
money. I have no say in that.

                    OLD LADY
                    (guffaws)
Do you also want me to call him up? I'm sure
he'll be interested to know why it's my daughter
in jail and not you.

Freda's stunned silence again reveals she is caught in another
lie.

                    OLD LADY
Oh. He doesn't know, does he?

                    FREDA
Leave now, please.

The baby cries again. The woman rises and heads for the door.

                    OLD LADY
          My money by the end of the month. And don't you
          think of running away again. If you got away the
          first time, I can assure you won't this time.

The baby cranks up the tears.

                    OLD LADY
          Go. Attend to your…baby.

BEDROOM - LATER

FREDA scoops up the baby and is mollified after feeling the
tense warmth of her shoulders. She presses him tightly against
her chest, as if casting off the fear raging inside her on him.

EXT. SHAW BOULEVARD - NIGHT

FREDDIE alights from a jeepney a few steps away from the street
where he lives.

A BABY POLICE SQUAD CAR seemingly tails him as he walks. He
tries to stay calm, not daring to look back at it. Shortly
after, the car cruises past him to his relief.

EXT. ANGELA'S HOUSE - LATER

All lights are out.

From a distance, FREDDIE scans for signs if the mother-and-son
nightmare could be watching his every move from the dark. He
hastens his steps home.

INT. APARTMENT - LATER

FREDDIE and FREDA are trying to work up an appetite to finish
their plates.

                    FREDDIE
          I bought a house.

                    FREDA
               (eyes beam as if she had

                    seen the light)
You did? When? Where?

                    FREDDIE
Today. In Valley Side Homes, Montalban.

                    FREDA
Montalban?!

                    FREDDIE
I know, I know. It's far from your mom.
                    (pause)
But if you want to keep that baby, we have to be
some place where no one knows us or about him.
And when we move, we can't tell anyone.

                    FREDA
What are we going to tell people when they
see us moving out our stuff?

                    FREDDIE
They won't. We leave everything behind
except for the clothes on our backs and those we
can fit in a luggage bag. We must leave at dawn.
When anyone spots us, we tell them we're on an
early flight to Hong Kong.

                    FREDA
And the baby?

                    FREDDIE
You were able to bring him out once unseen. I'm
sure you can think of something again.
          (pause)
So, what do you think?

                    FREDA
Okay, okay. Let's do it. I'll figure out what to
say to mommy later.

                    FREDDIE
Good.

                    FREDA
So, when do we move?

                              FREDDIE
                    End of the month.

                              FREDA
                    Perfect. That's just perfect.

EXT. THEIR STREET - DAY

FREDDIE thrusts himself out of the gate, his eyes trained on
ANGELA'S house. No sign of life inside. He skedaddles off.

INT. THEIR APARTMENT/LIVING ROOM - SAME DAY

All the lights are out, windows shut so as to give the
impression nobody's home.

POV BEDROOM - CONTINUOUS

A MAILMAN knocks on their door and announces that he's from the
Electric Company. The man knocks repeatedly.

FREDA -

Presses her finger against her lips to the baby lying in bed.

MAILMAN -

Gives up and slips the billing statement under the door.

BABY -

Laughs, sensing they have fooled the mailman.

She presses her nose on his for a job well done.

                              FREDA (VO)
                    Nice baby. Ready to get out of here?

INT. FREDDIE'S OFFICE - ANOTHER DAY

SUPER: 'End of the month. End of the 30-day Grace Period.'

FREDDIE'S CELL PHONE rings.

He fumbles and nearly drops it.

                    FREDDIE
          Hello? Annette! What's up?
                    (Long pause)
          What? Why? What's the problem?
                    (Tenses)
          The check? What about it?
                    (Pause)
          No way! What did the bank say?
                    (Distraught)
          Zero funds?! That's impossible. I'm sure it's
          just some glitch from their end.
                    (listens)
          Okay, okay. I'll take care of this.

INT. APARTMENT/ROOM- LATER

FREDDIE arrives to find FREDA zipping up their luggage. The baby
lies quietly in bed, dozing off.

                    FREDA
                    (startled)
          Whoa. I didn't hear you come in.
                    (checks the time on the wall)
          You're early. I thought you said we leave at
          11? Is there a cab waiting?

                    FREDDIE
          We're not going anywhere.

                    FREDA
          What?! What do you mean we're not moving?

                    FREDDIE
          My check bounced. Zero funds.

                    FREDA
          How did that happen?

FLASHBACK - OFFICE

PICK-UP from FREDDIE's phone conversation with a bank employee.

                    FREDDIE
          Hello? BPI? Yes, Trisha please.
                    (Long pause)
          Trisha? Hi. It's Freddie Mangahis.
          I was told there was a problem with my
          Valley Side check? Yes, for Valley Side
          Development.
                    (Long pause)
          What do you mean zero funds? How did that happen?
          Who made the withdrawal?
                    (Long pause)
          What other check? Who issued it?
                    (listens)
          To whom?
                    (listens)
          No. I don't know that person. Who issued it?

BACK TO FREDDIE AND FREDA -

                    FREDDIE
          Who is Amelita Boncayao?

                    FREDA
                    (Air escaping her)
          Sshhh-yet.

                    FREDDIE
          So, you know her. Who is this woman?
          What's going on?

FREDA spirals down in bed.

                    FREDA
          You remember Marissa, right? The one locked
          up in Jersey. That's her mom. Or so she said.
          She was here the other day. She accused me
          that I was the one who killed the baby and not
          her daughter.

                    FREDDIE
          So, she was trying to blackmail you?

                    FREDA
          Yeah. Something like that.

                    FREDDIE
          But does she have something on you?

She turns to the baby who remains unperturbed in his sleep.

                    FREDA
          Maybe.

                    FREDDIE
          What do you mean maybe?

                    FREDA
          I don't know, okay? Maybe.

                    FREDDIE
          Maybe?
                    (pause)
          Wait. Was it you who killed the baby?

                    FREDA
          Look, let's not do this now, okay?
          This is all so weird.

He slumps on the edge of the bed.

                    FREDDIE
                    (Exhaling tension)
          Wow. What a great, freakin' time for karma.

                    FREDA
          But that's not why she came here.
                    (Pause)
          She knows about the baby. And she knows
          about that Lotto money too.

                    FREDDIE
          What?! How?

                    FREDA
          Don't ask me how, okay? I have no idea.
          All I know is she knows. And she threatened
          to report us to the Baby Police if we don't
          pay up before the end of the month.

                    FREDDIE
          Wait. Did she also say end of the month?

                    FREDA
          Yes.
                    (pause)
          Wait. What do you mean also?

                    FREDDIE
          When did you issue the check?

                    FREDA
          I swear I never issued a check to her.
          That's why I agreed we leave before the end of
          the month... I have no intention of paying her a
          single cent. How she was able to fake our check
          is beyond me.

He crashes on his back like a chopped tree.

                    FREDDIE
          I don't freakin' believe this.

                    FREDA
          Wait. Didn't you say two checks cleared?
          What's the other one for?

Trapped, he slowly gets to a sitting position, trying to summon
the words from his lips.

                    FREDDIE
          Have you seen the one that just moved in?

                    FREDA
          Who moved in?

                    FREDDIE
          She was the one who saw you the other day.
          With the bag. And she knew what was inside it.
          Just like your blackmailer, she knew about the
          Lotto money and threatened to squeal to the
          Poos if I don't pay up by the end of the month.

                    FREDA
          Who's she? Do I know her? Do you know her?
                    (Remembers something)

Wait is it that woman living across the
street with a boy?

                    FREDDIE
So, you've seen them?

                    FREDA
Yes. Vaguely. Why? Who is she?

                    FREDDIE
               (Nods)
Angela. My ex from Cebu.

                    FREDA
You had an ex from Cebu? When did this happen?

                    FREDDIE
Seventeen years ago. Long before I met you. It
was my first provincial assignment.

                    FREDA
Did you knock her up?

                    FREDDIE
               (winces, as if he's been splashed with
               ice water)
I wasn't ready yet.
               (breathes hard)
Instead I volunteered to shoulder for
her abortion.

                    FREDA
Omigosh.

She stands up, paces the floor and settles on the opposite edge
of the bed.

                    FREDA
You were willing to kill your own kid?
I can't believe I'm hearing this.

                    FREDDIE
But it never happened, okay?
I just found out recently. She chose to
have the baby.
               (pause)
That's the boy you saw with her.

                    FREDA
Wait. So, are you saying the other half of our
money went to them?

                    FREDDIE
No. I don't know. I swear to you I wasn't giving
them a cent. I don't know how they pulled it off.

                    FREDA
Omigosh. This is like Twilight Zone karma.
          (pause)
So, what do we do now?

                    FREDDIE
There's only one thing left to do.
          (pause)
It's the thirtieth day. That baby has to go.

                    FREDA
That's your big idea?

                    FREDDIE
It's what we agreed on, remember?
          (pause)
Can't you see what's going on here?

                    FREDA
What?

                    FREDDIE
Just think of why that baby was given to us. It's
to make us pay for our sins, that's what. All
this s- -t happening to us, this is just the
beginning. Who knows how much worse it can get
the longer he stays with us?

                    FREDA
Yeah. Sure. Think what you think.
That seems easy enough for you.
You know why? Babies are like disposable
diapers to you. If you thought about killing your
own child, surely, what's to stop you from
dumping this one that didn't come from you.

                    FREDDIE
Ha! Really? This coming from one who actually

killed a child?

                    FREDA
Oh, screw you! That was an accident.
                    (pause)
I loved that kid like he was my own.
                    (tears up)
I would never do anything to hurt him.

Baby is roused and bawls. She scoops up the kid and rocks him in
her arms. Freddie considers turning on the boom box but lets it
go. Let this kid cry and screw them both.

                    FREDDIE
Look, I'm sorry.
                    (pulls her to sit next to him; puts
                    arm around her)
I shouldn't have said that.

                    FREDA
I just wanted to come home to you. I didn't
want to go to jail.

                    FREDDIE
I know. I know.
                    (pause)
So, what do we do now?

                    FREDA
I don't want to lose this baby.

                    FREDDIE
Hon, we can't do that. Not now.
                    (pause)
We have no money. We have nowhere to go.
And we can't keep him a secret any longer.
                    (pause)
I know how much he means to you. But he's not
ours. He's not our life. No matter what happens,
we still have each other.

                    FREDA
No. This baby... he's my life now.
                    (pause)
                    FREDDIE
Hon…

                    FREDA
          Look, when God gave me cancer, I didn't ask him
          to heal me. Just a chance to show I do care about
          that baby's life.
                    (pause)
          When this kid came, I knew that was His answer.
          It was Him saying He knows how much I care. This
          baby didn't just take away my cancer. He took
          away my guilt. He made me believe I wasn't a bad
          person after all. And if there's one miracle this
          baby did, it is to make me believe I can be a
          really terrific mom.
                    (pause)
          I'm sorry, dad. I love you. But I really can't
          give up this baby. Not to the Poos, not the
          government, not even his real mother. Let them
          come after me.

                    FREDDIE
          What are you going to do?

She rises, picks up the same gym bag from one corner and dumps
it on the bed. She presses her finger against her lips and
shushes the baby. The baby stops as if responding to her behest.
Then gingerly, she places him inside the bag.

                    FREDA
          You're right. We can't keep this secret
          any longer.
                    (pause)
          But if he goes...then I go.

                    FREDDIE
          Hon, don't be stupid.

The baby giggles. She zips up the bag and heads for the stairs.

                    FREDDIE
          Where do you think you're going?

                    FREDA
          I don't know. And I don't care.

She goes down the stairs without looking back. He doesn't
attempt to stop her. As the front door closes behind her, he
hears the baby cackling triumphantly.

LIVING ROOM - ANOTHER NIGHT

FREDDIE hardly has any appetite for his take-away dinner. In the
sink, Freda's coffee cup remains unwashed.

He turns on the TV. He hears the WANG-WANGING of a Baby Police
car siren in the distance. He gets unsettled, trying to shake
off thoughts that she could be in one of those cars already.

ON TV - THE NIGHTLY NEWS

                         FEMALE NEWSCASTER
               All's well that ends well for Melissa and her
               missing baby AM. She couldn't believe her ears
               when the Infant Crime Unit broke the good news
               that she was going to be reunited with her
               adopted one.

                                        CUT TO:

NEWS FOOTAGE - INFANT CRIME PRECINT

MELISSA, AM's mom, flanked by the Baby Police is swarmed by
reporters as she enters the Infant Crime Unit premises.

                         FEMALE NEWSCASTER (VO)
               It all began that morning when the Infant Crime
               Unit received a call from a concerned citizen.
               The caller reported spotting a woman, late 30's
               to early 40's, wandering around the food court of
               a popular shopping mall with baby in tow. Without
               doubt, the caller identified the baby in the
               woman's arms as the missing AM.

                                        CUT TO:

INTERVIEW WITH SAID FEMALE CALLER

                         CONCERNED CITIZEN
               I was a few tables away, but I kept an eye on her
               while I contacted the Infant Crime Unit. She must
               have spotted me and sensed what I was doing. She
               got up from her table, didn't even finish her

food then headed straight for the comfort room. I
didn't want to alarm her, so I didn't follow
immediately. When she stepped out of the CR, the
baby was no longer with her. So, I rushed to the
CR and there was a commotion of sorts. The woman
had left the baby there. Good thing the Baby
Police came right away. They scanned the
child and confirmed that it was indeed the
missing baby.

                                    CUT TO:

FOOTAGE - INFANT CRIME PRECINT

The Baby Police, before the media cams, turn AM over to his mom.
She hugs him tight and smothers him with kisses.

                                    CUT TO:

INTERVIEW - AM'S MOM

She beams before reporters, baby in her arms.

                    AM'S MOM
            We want to thank everyone, most especially
            the Infant Crime Unit for helping us recover my
            precious AM, safe and sound. This is truly a
            miracle.

FREDDIE -

Now, just two inches away from the moniror. He takes one look at
the recovered baby and realizes this AM doesn't look anywhere
close to their AM.

ON TV -

Hazy CCTV footage of the suspected woman, back on cam and baby
entering the CR. Her head is bowed as if conscious there are
electronic eyes on her.

                    NEWSCASTER
            As of this report, the Baby Police still
            have no clues as to the whereabouts of AM's
            kidnapper.

BEDROOM- LATER

FREDDIE lies sleepless in bed. He hears several more Baby Poo
cars wang-wang and wheezing in the distance. It's quite possible
one of those squad cars could be on their way to his apartment
unit and ready to break his door down.

MONTAGE -

1) Finally, he washes Freda's previously unwashed mug and places
   this next to his matching mug.

2) In the office, he busies himself to brush off any thoughts of
   her and the baby.

EXT. ANGELA'S HOUSE - NIGHT

It is dark and empty.

ANGELA'S GATE - CONTINUOUS

FREDDIE draws near the gate and peers inside.

                         FREDDIE
                  Angela? Angela!

He bangs the gate.

A MALE NEIGHBOR creeps up from behind him.

                         NEIGHBOR
             Hey you. You're looking for someone there?

                         FREDDIE
             Angela. The one who just moved in here.
             She has a son? You've never seen them?

                         NEIGHBOR
             Are you high? That house has been empty
             for two years.

                        FREDDIE
          What? Are you sure?

Another MALE NEIGHBOR passing by joins in.

                        NEIGHBOR 2
          Hey guys what's up?

                        NEIGHBOR
          You tell him. You're the caretaker here.

                        NEIGHBOR 2
          Tell him what?

                        FREDDIE
          A mother and his son just moved in here
          Have you seen them? Her name's Angela.

                        NEIGHBOR 2
          Angela who? If anyone's living there I should
          be the first to know. The owners entrusted
          that to us precisely to make sure no squatters
          break in.

                        FREDDIE
          Huh? So, you're saying…

                        NEIGHBOR 2
          I am saying this is a small neighborhood. If
          anyone even attempts to jump over that gate, I
          have everyone on full alert.

                        NEIGHBOR
          Look at him. He looks like he's seen a ghost.
          Or ghosts.

                        NEIGHBOR 2
          You see what happens when you stop hanging out
          with us? You get Vitamin Beer deficiency.

INT. ROOM - NIGHT

COMPUTER SCREEN - FACEBOOK:

FRIEND SEARCH PAGE - All those listed as ANGELA LOPEZ. Not a single one posted a pic.

FREDDIE -

Reclining in bed with laptop on his belly. He closes laptop and places it on Freda's empty bed space.

NEXT DAY -

Loud banging downstairs. FREDDIE rocks up from sleep. Could that be the Baby Police? The knocking persists though growing weaker after each interval.

LIVING ROOM - CONTINUOUS

He nervously approaches the door.

                    FREDDIE
          Who is it?

A familiar voice mumbles from behind the door. He opens it with a sigh of relief -

FREDA -

All worn out and in the same set of clothes when she left.

Two things are obviously missing from her.

The gym bag.

And the baby.

Their tired, however reconciling eyes lock. Freddie takes her hand and gently leads her inside.

ROOM - LATER

She is standing before the mirror and probing her chest.

INT.MALL - FLASHBACK

FREDA wanders around listlessly, gym bag slung on her shoulder.
Fatigue saddles her shoulders.

She parks herself on a chair outside a donut shop and observes
the mothers strolling by with their infants in tow. But what
really tugs her strings are the couples being amorous to each
other wheezing past her. She misses Freddie.

Startled SCREAMS erupt. A MAN streaks and slices through the
thick throng of people from nowhere, his arms tightly wrapped
around a baby.

Hot on his tail are two BABY POLICE officers.

Freda slings the bag on her shoulders as she rises from the
chair. A TEEN BOY, eyes nailed on his cell phone SLAMS into her
bag, jogging it. Like any typical ill-mannered teen possessed by
his gadget, the kid scurries away with nary an apology, as if
the person he just smacked into was some fixture. She cuts loose
a string of invectives at him. The kid pays her no mind, what
with his earphones drowning out her outrage.

She slowly unzips her bag and peers inside. At least her "cargo"
was hardly perturbed by all that sound and motion.

She starts to walk away, heading in the direction opposite where
the Baby Police and the suspected baby thief had continued their
chase.

Then a face in the crowd pops in front of her. It's her FRIEND
from New Jersey that Freddie ran into one time.

                    FRIEND
          Hey girl! I thought that was you.

She scans her face, as if having difficulty placing her.

                    FRIEND
          It's Lydia, you nut!

                    FREDA
          Omigosh, you! You look like you just bought
          a house in Forbes. How are you?

                    FRIEND
          Ha-ha, *bruha*. I wish. How are you?

I saw your husband one time. Did he tell you?

                FREDA
Yes, he did.

                FRIEND
So, you know what happened to Marissa?

                FREDA
I know. That's…that's really sad. She
going to prison.

                FRIEND
What?! Omigosh girl. That's not what I told him.

                FREDA
No?

                FRIEND
No. She never went to prison.
She's been cleared of all charges. She was
not the guilty one at all.

                FREDA
What? So, who is?

                FRIEND
Huh, it's complicated. Turns out the baby died
due to a wrong prescription for his cough and
fever. It triggered some allergic reaction that
caused complications. Marissa's attorney
convinced the court to have another coroner
review the autopsy. And that's what came
out in his findings. So, there you go.
She's coming home next month.

                FREDA
Really? That's great.
                (pause)
So, her mother must be so happy.

                FRIEND
What?! Which planet do you live in?
Her mother passed away five years ago.
We were all there when they buried her.
Wait. Weren't you there?

                    FREDA
          No. I don't remember. I don't think so.

                    FRIEND
          Oh wait. That's right. You were already in
          the US by then. Well, plenty to catch up
          on. Let's get together when she gets back.

                    FREDA
          Sure. I'd love that.

                    FRIEND
          How's Freddie? Where is he?

Tears well up in Freda's eyes. Friend notices the bag and puts
the pieces together. She had probably split from him.

MALL COMFORT ROOM - LATER

FREDA has the room all to herself. She enters one of the
cubicles then locks it.

She parks on the toilet seat then lands the bag on her lap. She
keeps an ear to the door. It seems no other lady urgently needs
to relieve herself. It seems fate is conspiring with what she
needs to do next. She gingerly unzips the bag.

The baby is beaming at her. She pulls him out, lands the bag by
her feet and then settles the baby on her lap.

The child breaks into hearty giggles. She draws him close to her
face, gently nudges her nose on his forehead and then planting a
kiss on his cheek. The child's hand reaches for her face and
wipes the tear that just rolled out her eye.

                    FREDA
          Baby…I think I made a mistake.
                    (pause)
          I can't do this anymore.
                    (pause)
          I need to go home.
                    (pause)
          I want to go home now.
                    (pause)
          I'm sorry…
                    (pause)

But I can't take you with me.

She plants another kiss on him. The still giggling baby hoists his hand. It LIGHTS UP like a bulb. He reaches out and touches her chest.

She feels life is getting sucked out of her.

                         FREDA
            Baby? W-wh…

FREDA'S POV -

Baby starts to get foggy, then whirly and then -

FADE TO WHITE

The blurry focus gets sharper to reveal -

FREDA'S FACE -

Her eyes pop open as she hears -

Hands BANGING on her cubicle door.

Her heart thumps. She refuses to open it. Someone kicks it open.

A JANITOR and a MALL GUARD glare at her, looking less suspicious than concerned.

                         JANITOR
            Ma'am, are you alright? You've been there
            for a long time.

                         MALL GUARD
            Can we call someone for you? Would you like us
            to take you to a hospital?

She shakes head no to both queries. Her foot brushes against the bag to feel it. Her heart nearly leaps out of her chest as she realizes something. The baby is no longer with her.

She furtively probes into the bag, careful not to alert the mall personnel what she's looking for. The baby is not there.

> MALL GUARD
> Did you lose anything?

She thrusts her body forward, swivels both ways to check before kicking the bag away from her.

> SECURITY GUARD
> Did you lose anything?

> FREDA
> Ah..No. Thank you.

END OF FLASHBACK - FREDA BY THE MIRROR

She raises her shirt slowly, wincing at the possibility of what she might see. Freddie's voice from below stops her.

> FREDDIE (OS)
> Hon...chow time.

DINING TABLE - LATER

It's quiet at the breakfast table. You can sense questions want to burst out of them but none wants to initiate the conversation. It's as if they feel any exchange of words might just ruin this moment. Instead, they trade smiles and quietly finish their meal.

INT. PASTOR'S HOUSE - ANOTHER NIGHT

SUPER: "Two Years After"

The ladies' D-group is gathered around their usual table. The men are conducting their own discussion in a separate dining area.

> PASTOR'S WIFE
> Good news, anyone? Any praise report? Anyone?

FREDA raises her hand, grinning ear to ear.

                    PASTOR'S WIFE
          Yes Freda? We're really glad you're back.

                    LADY 1
          Yeah. What happened to you?

                    FREDA
          A lot actually. But Praise God for your
          prayers. I'm happy to announce that…

FLASHBACK - FREDA BY THE MIRROR

She raises her shirt, eyes shut in fearful anticipation of what
could probably lie beneath.

With her shirt fully raised, she slowly opens her eyes.

Her breasts are as SMOOTH as a well-paved road. There are no
cancerous nodules as she had dreaded.

                    FREDA (VO)
          I have been cancer-free for two years now.

BACK TO LADIES' GROUP -

Thunderous applause. Profuse "Praise God" around the table.

MEN'S CORNER -

The loud celebration from the ladies got the men swinging to
their corner.

                    PASTOR
          Wow! What's the story over there?

FREDDIE raises his hand.

                    PASTOR
          Yes, Freddie? Care to enlighten us?

                    FREDDIE
          Yes. By the grace of God…

EXT. OFFICE - FLASHBACK

FREDDIE swivels in his executive chair in his own office. He
looks out the window where he has a panoramic view of the metro.

                    FREDDIE (VO)
          Last year, I got a new job. A much better one.
          With much better pay. But there's more. Just two
          months in, I got a commendation from my boss.
          He's putting me on the fast track for a
          promotion. But there's more…

EXT. UPPER MIDDLE-CLASS NEIGHBORHOOD - NIGHT - FLASHBACK

It's remote, inaccessible by public transportation, but quiet
and decent and dotted with condominium buildings and strip
commercial centers.

FREDDIE strolls through this street alone. Somewhere, we hear
the SIRENS of the Baby Poo vans, perhaps dealing with another
night of baby theft and baby piracy. He couldn't care less.

                    FREDDIE (VO)
          Freda also closed a sale she had been working on
          for months. We couldn't believe it. The
          commission was really huge.

He walks up to the entrance of a newly constructed CONDOMINIUM.
The geezer GUARD by the entrance scans him.

                    FREDDIE (VO)
          It was more than enough for a huge down payment
          for a condo.

The old GUARD recognizes him. He smiles and salutes him.

BACK TO MEN'S GROUP -

The men erupt with their own thunderous applause and "Praise
God."

                    PASTOR
          Amazing! What a tremendous blessing. When
          God works, he really works wonders.

                    FREDDIE
          So true. And he adds no troubles to it like he
          promised.

                    PASTOR
          So, when are you inviting us to the
          housewarming?

BACK TO LADIES' GROUP -

They're all abuzz about FREDA'S blessing.

                    FREDA
               Actually, there's another thing I want to share…

INT. CONDO UNIT - FLASHBACK

FREDDIE saunters into the unit which he now calls home. It's
simple yet elegant.

He heads straight to the dining table where a mini- buffet
spread is waiting for him.

He forks a generous heap of one of the viands and wolfs it down.

                    FREDDIE
          Hon…

                    FREDA (OC)
          I'm here.

He walks up to -

THEIR BALCONY - CONTINUOUS

FREDA is leaning against the rail sucking in the breath-taking
sights of the metro skyline at night.

                    FREDDIE
          What's with all the food? Are we expecting
          anyone? What are we celebrating?

She turns to him as if unable to convey what's on her mind.

>   FREDDIE
>   Something wrong?

>   FREDA
>   (smiles)
>   Actually...we are expecting something else.

>   FREDDIE
>   Really? What?

She takes his hand and lands it on her belly. He doesn't get it
at first. But as her smile widens, he finally realizes what's
happening.

His eyes light up, as if inquiring if what he conjectures is
true. She nods vigorously then wraps her arms around him.

FADE TO BLACK

CLOSING CREDITS

A MAN OF FAUXIBILITIES

Natzee AB is a Story Slinger from the Philippines. He is also the author of the Fauxibility Series of books, TWEETLIT, FAUXGASM, and TRES BAYANI & THE CUP NOODLE, the first volume of a three-volume set dubbed HEROIC FAUXIBILITIES. His writing mojo was engineered by God and juiced up by years of crafting ad copy and dabbling in screenplays. The latter earned him a finals berth in the Manila Hollywood Pitchmart contest. He credits God, the Greatest Storyteller of all, long followed by Vonnegut, King and Murakami, among others for launching his Fauxible Adventures. He is happily married to his Chummie Cloude and Numero Uno fan and critic of 25 years, Therese Bridget Angeles. While laying the groundwork for his next books, he is also busy fulfilling his duties as caregiver, nurse, therapist, cook, and above all, devoted husband to his convalescent spouse who suffered a mild stroke.

CPSIA information can be obtained
at www.ICGtesting.com
Printed in the USA
LVHW052040260720
661580LV00015B/620

9 781952 011054